THE DEBS OF
BLETCHLEY PARK

Michael Smith is an award-winning journalist and the author of a number of bestselling books on spies, special forces and codebreaking, including *The Sunday Times* number one bestseller *Station X: The Codebreakers of Bletchley Park*; *Foley: The Spy Who Saved 10,000 Jews* and *The Emperor's Codes: Bletchley Park's Role in the War Against Japan*. He is also the editor of *The Secret Agent's Bedside Reader* and co-editor, with Ralph Erskine, of *The Bletchley Park Codebreakers*. Smith was a member of the British Army's Intelligence Corps before joining the BBC. He was a reporter and defence correspondent for both the *Daily Telegraph* and *The Sunday Times*, covering the wars in the Balkans, Iraq and Afghanistan. Smith is a trustee of Bletchley Park, the chair of the Trust's Historical Advisory Committee and one of the judges for the St Ermin's Hotel Intelligence Book of the Year.

THE DEBS OF
BLETCHLEY PARK

BY MICHAEL SMITH

Aurum
Press

First published in Great Britain
2015 by Aurum Press Ltd
74–77 White Lion Street
Islington
London N1 9PF

www.aurumpress.co.uk

This paperback edition first published in 2015 by Aurum Press Ltd

A catalogue record for this book is available from the British Library.

ISBN 978 1 78131 589 7

1 3 5 7 9 10 8 6 4 2

2015 2017 2019 2018 2016

Typeset in ITC New Baskerville by SX Composing DTP, Rayleigh, Essex

Printed by in Denmark by Nørhaven, Viborg

Contents

Prologue

Roma Davies lives in Bower Mount Road, to the west of Maidstone. It's one of those spacious tree-lined streets of elegant Edwardian villas that the estate agents like to call desirable. Roma has lived here for most of her life, ever since she and Mike finally got married.

They met at the end of the war. He'd been on the Arctic convoys taking food and equipment to Russia, sailing around the north of Norway to Archangel. They lost sixteen Royal Navy ships and eighty-five merchant vessels to the U-boats. God knows how many men. If you went into the sea it was so cold you were dead within minutes. Roma was in the navy herself back then, a member of the Women's Royal Naval Service, known to all and sundry as the Wrens.

'Mike and I wanted to get married but we didn't for ages because his mother said no.' Roma laughs. 'We were ruled by our parents. It's extraordinary to think of it now. I've never been able to be the boss. My daughters say, "You must be joking, Mum!" But I never was the boss.'

When she left the Wrens, she wanted to work in horti-culture. She loves plants. Her father didn't think that was a proper job for a young woman and sent her on a Pitman's secretarial course. Working as a typist was the sensible thing to do; it would bring in money straightaway. So Roma got a job at the Alliance Building Society offices on London's Park Lane.

When she and Mike did eventually get married in 1951, they moved into a rented cottage at the southern end of Bower Mount Road. When their first daughter was two, with Mike working as an engineer on reasonably good money, they bought one of those elegant Edwardian villas with large bay windows, a beautiful arched porch and the longest garden you could ever imagine. It was to be Roma's home for more than fifty years.

'It was a lovely house: lovely big garden; lots of happy memories; lots of friends. Sadly, they're all dying off now.'

Mike's heart gave way in 1996 and after Roma's second stroke, her daughters persuaded her she couldn't live on her own. She moved into the Grove, another of those Edwardian houses that line Bower Mount Road, and even more spacious than Roma's house. The Grove is a residential home for the elderly.

Roma sits in a tall-backed armchair in her room. It's about the size of a small hotel suite. There are photographs of her family, a few small pieces of furniture, and some paintings and ornaments she brought from her old home. They include two beautiful Royal Doulton figurines and a pretty watercolour of her grandmother's old house that reminds Roma of her childhood. She smiles a lot. She seems happy and the people at the Grove are kind and caring. A chirpy, friendly carer pops in to bring her tea and a piece of cake. It's someone's birthday. The two women laugh at a misunderstanding over the sugar, comfortable in each other's company. Roma is definitely happy here, you can tell. She's smiling a lot, and laughing.

Even so. The Grove might be in Bower Mount Road, but it isn't Roma's home. Not her real home. Not that the old house she and Mike lived in is hers any more – it was sold to pay for her care. It's someone else's now, to do with as they please. For a brief moment, the smile disappears.

'They've completely destroyed my front garden. The house was built in 1906. It's more than a hundred years old. There were all sorts of treasures in that garden, a hundred years of treasures, and they've just ripped them out and made a huge car park.'

The smile, though, is never far away.

There's a photograph of a pretty young woman in Wren's uniform. She's standing outside an old country house, smiling at the camera, a very pretty smile. Her hands are clasped contentedly in front of her. She looks happy . . . and very proud.

'I was determined to be a Wren from when I was at school. I couldn't wait to get into the Wrens. I wanted to do my bit. We were brought up to be patriotic.'

Roma's family lived in Leigh-on-Sea, Essex, before the war. Roma's mother loved being by the sea, as did Roma. In the summer, she and her brother would rush out of school at lunchtime and take a taxi down to the beach to have a picnic with their mother before taking another taxi back to school. But in the summer of 1939, everybody knew there was going to be a war with Hitler's Germany.

Roma's father thought the Thames Estuary would be the first place to be bombed, so he packed the entire family off to Devon.

'Three days before war broke out we moved down to my great-aunt's in Exeter. There was my brother, my sisters, my grandmother, two aunts and their children. It was a huge house, but we soon filled it up.' She laughs again and then the smile is back, the same pretty smile in the photograph. 'I was very sheltered. It wasn't until we went down into town that I even realised we were at war.'

As soon as she was seventeen, Roma rushed down to the local WRNS recruiting office to sign up, returning dejected to school after being told that seventeen wasn't old enough. You had to be seventeen and a half.

Six months later, Roma was a Wren. She trained at Mill Hill in north London, expecting to be posted somewhere by the sea, but to her disappointment she was sent just a few miles down the road to a new base at Eastcote where everything was secret. She was working with a lot of other Wrens on weird machines, with no real idea of what any of them were doing, or why. Except everything they did had to be done very quickly. Lives depended on it, so they did precisely what they were told.

'I had no idea of the overall picture and no notion of what my friends were doing,' she recalls.

When they had days off, they took the Tube into London and had fun, or simply something to eat that was different from navy rations.

'We were often treated because we were in uniform. The manager of a cinema would say: "Oh, let them in." We'd go to the Variety Club, and see comedians, dancers and singers – decent ones. We'd eat in Lyons Corner Houses, nothing special, baked beans on toast, that sort of thing. We were paid the princely sum of nine shillings [45p] a week. We had quite a few meals each week on that nine shillings. Incredible really how we made it last.'

After a few months, they told Roma they had a new job for her, somewhere north of London. She'd be living in much more comfortable conditions, in an old country mansion, and she'd be working at somewhere very, very secret, even more secret than Eastcote. Roma was to be one of the thousands of young women who spent their war carrying out work vital to the war effort, but never able to confide in anyone about it.

She would be working at Bletchley Park.

1

The Biggest Lunatic Asylum in Britain

Phoebe Senyard was not very happy. She was packing up all the office files and equipment into tea chests. Phoebe had only just returned from a holiday with her mother to be told she was being sent to the 'War Station' at Bletchley Park the very next day. She and Commander Crawford were to be the entire German naval codebreaking section. They weren't the only ones going, of course, but the Navy had insisted that the Government Code and Cypher School's real German Naval Section must stay in London, sat in the Admiralty, so she and Commander Crawford were going to be the only German naval 'experts' at Bletchley. Phoebe was no codebreaker and she certainly wouldn't regard herself as a German expert. She didn't understand how anyone would. She'd originally been recruited as a clerk and knew very little about the German 'Enigma' codes. Not that anyone else seemed to understand them either.

It was August 1939. Everybody knew that a war with Hitler was just around the corner. But no one had done much about the German codes. Admiral Sir Hugh Sinclair, who as chief of the secret service was in charge of the spies and the codebreakers, didn't believe the German codes would be broken. They were too modern, too complex. Ciphers produced by a machine, not by people. How could you break them without the machine? Commander Alastair Denniston, the head of the Government Code and Cypher School, agreed with the admiral. He usually did. Only Dilly Knox seemed to believe that Enigma could be broken. Phoebe was in no position to say whether the admiral or Mr Knox was right. She'd been picked out as one of the clerical workers who might be capable of doing a bit more, and once a week or so, if she was up to date with her own work, she helped Miss Yeoman register the naval Enigma messages. But there was very little else that anyone could do with them other than note down the main details, put them in the right order and then stack them away in a filing cabinet. No one thought there would ever be a chance of breaking them. Not even Mr Knox, and he was the Enigma expert. They were far too complex, even more complex than the German army and air force Enigma messages. Well, that's what Sheila Yeoman said.

But the more pressing problem was her mother. Who would look after her? Phoebe was forty-eight, a member of that generation of women who'd watched the men they loved march off to the trenches, some never to return. For many, it signalled the end of any hope of raising a family of their own. All Phoebe had now was her mother

– and her younger brother Henry – and Mother was in her seventies. That's why the job at Broadway Buildings had been so handy, a short train trip from Peckham Rye to Victoria and then a five-minute walk into work. Bletchley was much further away. Phoebe knew, of course, that if there was a war, there would have to be sacrifices. But she had responsibilities. Her father had died three years earlier, leaving just the three of them. But Henry was still a young man and if there was another war he was bound to be called up. What would become of Mother then? So it was with some trepidation, or as Phoebe put it, 'fear and trembling', that she agreed to go.

'I did try to protest but I was told that it was only for a fortnight so I gave in.' Not only was she going to have to leave Mother on her own but no one seemed able to tell her what she would be doing. 'A great deal of secrecy had to be observed, of course. I think Commander Crawford was overawed by the secrecy and was afraid to discuss the work with me at all.'

Secrecy and codebreaking went hand in hand. The British had been breaking the codes of their enemies, and very often their friends as well, since the fourteenth century. Letters sent back to Paris, Madrid and Rome by the ambassadors of France, Spain and the Vatican were intercepted and read on the orders of King Edward II. The British intercept operations were secret but the ambassadors soon realised what was going on and began writing their letters in code. Elizabeth I's spymaster Sir Francis Walsingham wasn't going to let that stop him finding out what the Queen's enemies were planning.

He set up a codebreaking operation run by the Queen's astrologer John Dee, whose predictions suddenly became so accurate that the Spanish Governor of the Netherlands complained that his reports for the King of Spain were being read in London before they even reached Madrid.

Oliver Cromwell went further, placing a 'Secret Man' in the Post Office to intercept and read the letters of suspected opponents of his government, with Parliament backing the scheme 'to discover and prevent many dangerous and wicked designs'. Before long, the 'Secret Man' had become a 'Secret Department' controlled by the Foreign Office with its own 'Secret Deciphering Branch', but when news of its extensive operations inside Britain emerged in the mid-1800s it was closed down.

The Great War, as Phoebe and her colleagues would still have called it, and the use of the new 'wireless apparatus' for military communications, revived the need for code-breakers. Wireless messages could be intercepted by the enemy, so the important ones had to be sent in code. Both the Royal Navy and the British Army set up wireless sites to intercept German messages and recruited university professors to decode them. Commander Denniston was in charge of Room 40, as the Admiralty codebreakers were known, from the room in the Old Admiralty Buildings that they occupied. Dilly Knox, a noted classical scholar, was one of its leading lights, decoding a lot of important German messages, including the one that brought the Americans into the war in 1917.

When the Great War came to an end, the army and navy codebreaking organisations were combined into the

Government Code and Cypher School and began breaking American, Japanese and Russian codes. The American and Japanese navies were seen as the main threat to Britain's domination of the seas and the Russians were dangerous Bolsheviks intent on overthrowing Western democracy. The Germans didn't feature in the codebreakers' list of targets. They were assumed to have been beaten once and for all. It was only after Adolf Hitler came to power in 1933 that Dilly began to work on the Enigma codes. He managed to break the Spanish and Italian versions, but the German Enigma messages were impossible to crack.

By now the Code and Cypher School had been taken over by Admiral Sinclair and was based just across the road from St James's underground station in the headquarters of the Secret Intelligence Service, soon to acquire the title of MI6. The vast majority of the actual codebreakers were men, with women like Phoebe involved in menial tasks such as the basic registering of messages, typing or filing. There were a couple of female codebreakers, one of whom, Joan Wingfield, a pretty 26-year-old from Sheffield, had spent the early 1930s in Italy living with her Uncle Claude, the Lloyd's agent (and MI6 man) in Livorno. Joan soon became fluent in Italian. But in 1935 Uncle Claude was thrown out of Italy for spying and joined the Code and Cypher School as an Italian expert, bringing Joan in with him. She was soon decoding messages between Italian ships and their shore bases. But she was very much an exception. By and large the most responsible job given to a woman was as a translator. They were also paid substantially less than the men, around £200 a year for a junior civil servant compared to the male salary of £250. This was regarded as perfectly normal within the Civil Service and across industry at that time. The men would have families to support; the women didn't need so much money.

Barbara Abernethy joined at the age of sixteen, which meant she earned even less. She was from Belfast but had been educated at a convent in Belgium and was fluent in French, German and Flemish. In August 1937, when Commander Denniston was looking for a typist, she was transferred from the Foreign Office to Broadway where she was paid the grand sum of 31 shillings and 6d a week, just under £82 a year.

'I was posted over there not knowing what I was doing and told that it was strict secrecy. I was there for a week and they apparently approved of me because I was kept on and I stayed there.' Barbara worked with Phoebe and liked her a lot. 'She was very pretty, a very good-looking woman. She seemed terribly old to me but she must have been in her forties. Very nice, very pleasant face, very confident, everybody liked her.'

Not everyone was so universally liked as Phoebe. Many of the older codebreakers were eccentric personalities and difficult to handle, not least Dilly Knox, who threatened to resign at the slightest change in routine. When one of the codebreakers committed suicide, throwing himself under an underground train at Sloane Square station, Admiral Sinclair decided that working such clever men too hard 'overstrained their minds', and he ordered Commander Denniston to cut back their hours. They didn't have to start work until ten o'clock in the morning, had ninety minutes for lunch, and finished on the dot at five o'clock. Despite her low pay, Barbara thought it was wonderful.

'Life was very civilised in those days. We stopped for tea and it was brought in by messengers. I was very impressed by this, first job I'd ever had and it seemed paradise to me. Nice people and very interesting work. I thought, well, this is the life, isn't it. Thank God I'm not back in the Foreign Office.'

Many of the young women working for the Code and Cypher School were, like Barbara and Joan, from relatively well-to-do families, recruited because they knew someone who worked there, and were therefore deemed to be trustworthy. Diana Russell-Clarke's father Edward had worked with the codebreakers during the Great War; at the beginning of 1939, with war with Hitler on the horizon, she decided she needed to do something to defend Britain. Naturally, the first person she turned to for help in finding the right job was her mother. It was the normal thing for a young woman of Diana's class to do.

'My mother simply rang up Commander Denniston, whom we called Liza because we'd known him all our lives, and asked him: "Have you got a job for Diana?" He said, "Yes. Send her along." So that's where I started. We were decoding. But it was very, very boring, just subtracting one row of figures from another. We were on the third floor. There were MI6 people upstairs. They were always known as "the other side". We didn't have any truck with them.'

Concerned that his staff would be at risk if the Germans bombed London, the admiral had bought a country estate and mansion at Bletchley Park, far enough away from

London to be safe but linked to Whitehall via the main telephone communications cables that connected the capital with the far north. This was to be the 'War Station' for Britain's spies and codebreakers.

Phoebe, Joan, Barbara and Diana were among just over a hundred codebreakers who travelled to Bletchley Park in August 1939. Many went by train, instructed to make sure that they only bought a ticket that was 'of the appropriate class' for their status within the Code and Cypher School, which for Phoebe and Barbara was very definitely third class. A few, like Diana, were lucky enough to have cars and were encouraged to take them so they could help ferry people into work each day.

'A great friend lent me his Bentley for the duration of the war because he decided it was better for it to be driven than be put up on blocks. So I had this beautiful grey Bentley and of course the private cars were useful because we used to collect people to come into work and then drop them home afterwards.'

Initially they were all put up in pubs or hotels, where the mix of secretive elderly men and very young women, most of them much younger than Phoebe, scandalised the hotel staff, who assumed they must be up to no good. They weren't alone. The codebreakers weren't allowed to tell even their own family where they were, leading Barbara's mother to worry what her eighteen-year-old daughter might be doing.

'My mother didn't know where I was and I was reasonably young. She had to sort of trust. I told her these people were very respectable.'

The codebreakers were instructed to inform any locals inquisitive enough to ask that they were working on plans for the air defence of London. The servicemen attached to the Code and Cypher School's naval, military and air sections were ordered to wear civilian clothes. Bletchley Park was now to be known simply as 'Station X', not as a sign of mystery but simply the tenth of a number of stations owned by MI6 and identified by Roman numerals. All mail was to be sent to an anonymous Post Office box number in Westminster from where it would be collected and delivered to Bletchley by MI6 courier.

It wasn't just Phoebe who was promised they weren't going to be at Bletchley for very long. Barbara was told not to bring any more clothing than she would need for a two-week stay.

'It was pretty well organised. I was in the Bridge Hotel, Bedford. None of us quite knew what would happen next. War had not been declared and most people thought and hoped that nothing would happen and we would all go back to London.'

The Naval Section moved into the library and the loggia, a conservatory on the left-hand side of the mansion as you looked at it from the front. Phoebe's German section was in a corner of the library with two tables, a steel locker and a telephone with a direct line to the Admiralty. There were just two chairs, one each for her and Commander Crawford, but with the work piling up she soon had reinforcements.

'On 28 August 1939 we were joined by Misses Doreen Henderson and Cherrie Whitby and I need hardly say how welcome they were, for up to this time, we had only been helped by casual labour, some of it of the most doubtful kind, so that when they came we breathed a sigh of relief. Miss Whitby was as dark as Doreen was fair and they formed absolute contrasts to each other in appearance. Doreen came to help me with the registering and we became submerged under the spate of German intercepted signals which came pouring in, whilst Cherrie Whitby worked with Mrs Edwards, who was one of the temporary helpers. Both Doreen and Cherrie were excellent workers and were of great value to the section. We were very lucky in having such help.'

Admiral Sinclair paid for a good chef from one of the top London hotels to cook for them in the mansion and ensure they were properly fed. Despite concerns over her mother, Phoebe loved the 'wonderful lunches' the chef provided. 'Bowls of fruit, sherry trifles, jellies and cream were on the tables and we had chicken, hams and wonderful beef steak puddings. We certainly couldn't grumble about our food.'

Most of the codebreakers were from upper-class or upper middle-class backgrounds and were used to the fine dining and relaxed well-to-do atmosphere of the country estate. But for young women like Barbara, who by the standards of the day came from a relatively well-off family, it was a completely new experience, something she'd only read about in Agatha Christie novels.

'It was beautiful: lovely rose gardens, a maze, a lake, lovely old building, wonderful food.' For those brief two weeks in August 1939, Bletchley Park really did have the relaxed air of a weekend party at an English country mansion.

Then on Friday 1 September 1939, Hitler invaded Poland on the pretext of retaking German territory lost in the Great War and the Second World War began. Britain was not yet at war with Germany. The British Prime Minister Neville Chamberlain mobilised British troops and gave Hitler an ultimatum. Withdraw from Poland or Britain would declare war. Hitler had until eleven o'clock on the morning of Sunday 3 September to respond. At a quarter past eleven that Sunday morning, the codebreakers clustered around the wireless set in the mansion dining room to listen to what Mr Chamberlain had to say. He informed the nation that he was talking to them from the Cabinet Room in 10 Downing Street.

'This morning the British Ambassador in Berlin handed the German Government a final note stating that unless we heard from them by 11am that they were prepared at once to withdraw their troops from Poland, a state of war would exist between us. I have to tell you now that no such undertaking has been received, and that consequently this country is at war with Germany.'

The Prime Minister told the nation that he had fought for peace but Hitler wasn't interested in peace, only in the use of force, and as a result force was the only way to stop him. The situation in which no people or country could feel themselves safe in the face of German aggression had become intolerable and 'now that we have resolved to finish it, I know that you will all play your part with calmness and courage'. There would be 'days of stress and strain' ahead but it was vital that everyone pulled together and did their job.

Many of those listening were like Phoebe. They remembered the Great War, now forever destined to be known as the First World War, and they knew at first hand the sacrifices they had made, the loved ones lost. That was one of the reasons Chamberlain had bent over backwards in an attempt to avoid another war. The gist of his address to the nation that quiet Sunday morning was that Hitler had given them no choice. Britain might not want war, but it was doing the right thing. Quite unfairly, Chamberlain's name would become a byword for appeasement of Hitler. He was certainly not a man capable of rousing the nation in the manner of Winston Churchill, who would succeed him as Prime Minister the following May, but at the time his address was seen as both honest and, in its own modest way, suitably inspiring. He finished with the words: 'Now may God bless you all. May he defend the right. It is the evil things that we shall be fighting against – brute force, bad faith, injustice, oppression and persecution – and against them I am certain that the right will prevail.'

Britain was at war but it remained far from clear what the codebreakers' contribution might be. Dilly Knox still hadn't broken the German Enigma codes, although he was now very close to success, thanks to the Poles.

The Enigma cipher machine had been invented by a German company in the early 1920s, originally for use by banks and other commercial organisations that needed to keep data confidential. It was adopted by the German Navy in 1926 and two years later by the German Army. The machine itself looked rather like a typewriter encased in a wooden box. It had a keyboard and on top of the machine was a lampboard with a series of lights, one for every letter, laid out in the same order as the keyboard. The main internal mechanism was made up of three metal rotors, each with twenty-six electrical contacts around its circumference, one for every letter of the alphabet.

In order to encode the message, the operator set the rotors in a predetermined order and position, known as the settings. He then typed each letter of the message into the machine. The action of pressing the key sent an electrical impulse through the machine which passed through each of the rotors and lit up the encoded letter on the lampboard.

The machine didn't print anything out and it didn't send the message itself. The operator simply noted down the encoded letter from the lampboard and typed in each of the other letters until he had a completely encoded message which he sent via wireless, normally using Morse code.

As a letter was typed in the first rotor moved forward one position. After that rotor had moved a certain number of times, the second rotor moved forward once, and after the second rotor had moved a number of times, the third rotor moved once. As a result, the code was constantly changing with every letter. The Germans added a plug-board providing an additional level of security which they believed made Enigma unbreakable.

But they were wrong. The Poles, who shared a border with the Germans and had never stopped seeing them as a threat, had begun trying to break Enigma shortly after the Germans first started using it. The Polish codebreaking organisation, the *Bureau Szyfrow*, employed a group of mathematicians led by a young man called Marian Rejewski, who used mathematics to work out the internal wiring and mechanism of the German Army Enigma machine. He was helped by a spy inside the German War Ministry, an army colonel who provided the French with the Enigma settings and operations manual in return for money and sex; the French shared this intelligence windfall with the Poles. It certainly gave the Polish mathematicians the start they needed, but reconstructing the machine mathematically remained an amazing achievement.

For several years, the Poles managed to keep breaking Enigma, but as war approached and the German security systems improved it became increasingly difficult to decode and they approached the British, hoping they might be able to help. It took a while before the two sides trusted each other enough to share what they knew, but once Marian Rejewski and Dilly Knox were left alone to discuss their different methods of breaking codes, cooperation began in earnest.

Dilly Knox had in fact got very close to breaking the German Enigma messages himself. The main thing stopping him, the one thing he'd been unable to work out, was the way in which the letters of the keyboard were connected to the internal rotors. If he could only work that out, he would be able to read the German Enigma codes. One female codebreaker, a 'Mrs B', suggested that the simplest way to do it would be A to A, B to B, C to C, and so on. But that was a ridiculous idea. Scrambling the connections would make the code far more secure.

Any sensible person would want the links between the keyboard and the rotors to be completely random, making it far more difficult for people like Dilly to break. The Poles, however, told Dilly that it was in fact A to A, B to B, C to C . . . Mrs B had been right all along. The Germans had decided that since the electrical wiring was soldered into the machine by hand it would be too much of a risk to make the connections random. It would be too easy to make a mistake in the wiring. If it was as straightforward as A to A, B to B, there would be no doubt as to how the machine should be wired up. Given the extra security the Germans had put in place, knowing this still wasn't enough to get Dilly into the Enigma codes, but he knew now that he was very close.

Commander Denniston, who had travelled to Poland with Dilly to meet the Polish mathematicians, was understandably impressed by the Polish mathematicians' success in breaking Enigma. Dilly was a brilliant codebreaker, who had unravelled the mysteries of the bawdy comedies of the Greek poet and playwright Herodas from fragments of papyrus scrolls found in an Egyptian cave. He had shown himself adept at breaking every kind of code, including the Spanish and Italian Enigma codes, but when it came to the German Enigma he had not been as adept as the Poles.

In the months leading up to the war, Commander Denniston had toured Britain's universities, looking for professors and lecturers who might make good codebreakers. Initially, he targeted linguists and classicists, but after meeting the Poles he began to interview mathematicians. One of the first he recruited was a young Cambridge academic called Alan Turing who was making a name for himself with his ideas for 'a universal computing machine'. Admiral Sinclair authorised Commander Denniston to recruit fifty senior academics, both men and women, and thirty female language graduates. Although the tilt towards more women might seem a positive move, it was actually done on purely practical grounds. Young men were likely to be needed by the armed forces and women were far cheaper to employ.

All the academics were given some training in code-breaking and made to sign the Official Secrets Act. They were told to keep a ten-shilling note in their pockets at all times for a railway ticket and to wait for a telegram saying simply that 'Auntie Flo is unwell'. On receipt of the message, they were to make their way to Station X.

In the days following Chamberlain's declaration of war, the messages went out and the dons began arriving at Bletchley. The original codebreakers moved out of the hotels and into 'billets'. Local people with spare bedrooms were required to let them stay there in return for a guinea (£1.05) a week. Barbara Abernethy was put into a house belonging to the owner of a large chain of car dealerships.

'I was in a very nice billet to start with in a place called Great Brickhill and the dons were all in one pub up there called The Duncombe Arms. Since I lived in Great Brickhill, I was exposed to them more than most people early on. There were a lot of dons staying at the pub, about six or eight of them, all of them having such a jolly time that they called it the Drunken Arms.'

The first few months after September 1939 were known as

the Phoney War. Nothing seemed to be happening. British troops were sent to France but they weren't involved in any fighting. The Royal Navy did have a number of clashes at sea with German ships but at Bletchley only those people working on German material like Phoebe were busy.

'We were deluged with intercepted German messages which we still continued to register, although we really could not cope with it and were days behind. However, we struggled valiantly with it, each of us taking it in turns.'

Things began to turn around for Phoebe when Frank Birch, an actor and comic who had been in Room 40 during the First World War, arrived to take charge of the German Naval Section and had the rest of the section sent up from London.

'In no time, we were filing, sorting, making and receiving reports. None of us specialised. We all had to help one another and all who came to the section did a bit of everything.'

One of those helping Phoebe was Jocelyn Bostock, a 23-year-old German linguist from a wealthy, middle-class family in Hampstead. She went to Cheltenham Ladies' College, where she became head girl, and then read modern languages at Lady Margaret Hall, Oxford.

'Oxford in those days was an exciting place. I loved the old buildings, the boating on the river, the walks along the towpath. I travelled in France, Germany and Switzerland, staying in private families and acquiring fluency in two languages as well as a German boyfriend who wrote to me regularly until the outbreak of war.'

After working with Jewish children who had fled

Germany, Jocelyn was recruited to Bletchley Park on the recommendation of the principal of Lady Margaret Hall and allocated to the naval section, helping Phoebe to sort out the German naval messages.

Dilly Knox and the young, newly recruited mathematicians were busy in a cottage behind the mansion trying to break into the Enigma ciphers. But other sections had far less to do. The Italians and the Japanese hadn't entered the war yet. Barbara helped organise games of rounders after lunch to wear off the effects of the food and keep people amused.

'We had a tennis ball and somebody managed to commandeer an old broom handle, drilled a hole in it and put a leather strap in it. It was all we had, things were getting a bit tough to get. If it was a fine day, we'd all say rounders at one o'clock, we'd all go out and play, just to sort of let off steam. Everybody argued about the rules and the dons just laid them down, in Latin sometimes. That was the way they were.'

As more people arrived to deal with the German codes, Commander Denniston realised he had a problem. There was nowhere to put them all.

The admiral decided that wooden huts should be put up around the mansion to house the naval, air and military sections. There were already three huts which had been built for some of the MI6 sections before the codebreakers arrived. Hut 4 was constructed just outside the library, replacing the beautiful rose garden that had so entranced Barbara Abernethy. The new hut was designed to house the Air Section, but when they'd moved in and there were still a few empty rooms at one end, the German Naval Section was moved in there too, much to Phoebe's relief, initially at least.

'We had become very cramped in our quarters; files were increasing and the numbers of our personnel were slowly mounting so that the amount of space at our disposal had dwindled to such a degree that Jocelyn Bostock and I were working together on a small kitchen table and getting very much in one another's way, as one can imagine. Even the floor was used to sort signals and it must have been amusing to see us on all fours doing this job. It needs no great effort of the imagination to realise how very delighted we were to hear that we were to move into Hut 4.'

There might have been more space to work in the huts but, with their thin wooden walls and floors, they were far from comfortable and very cold. The glass of the windows was taped up to protect against bomb blasts and covered in blackout curtains. They were lit by bare light bulbs and kept warm at best by paraffin heaters, at worst by cast-iron coke stoves which Phoebe found impossible to light or control.

'They were awful. When the wind was high, long flames would be blown out into the room, frightening anyone nearby. Alternatively, the fire would go out and smoke would come billowing forth, filling the room with a thick fog and, with all the windows open to let out the smoke, the shivering occupant would be dressed in a thick overcoat, scarf and gloves, endeavouring to cope with his work.'

Across Britain there was very much a patriotic spirit, inspired by the Prime Minister's address to the nation.

There was a genuine feeling that Britain was doing the right thing, taking on the evil of Hitler and the Nazi regime. Women inevitably had much more of a role in society than they had become used to between the wars. Even for those whose fathers, husbands or sweethearts were not already serving in the forces, there was a realisation that it would be inevitable and, as had been the case during the First World War, women would have to keep the country running while the men went abroad to fight. The Women's Voluntary Services for Air Raid Precautions was set up in early 1938, working in close association with the Women's Institute. Amid fears of German bombing raids on the major cities, young mothers often experienced the effects of war before their husbands, suffering the emotional turmoil of having their children evacuated to the countryside. When their husbands were called up they found themselves looking for some way of 'doing their bit'.

Most women felt very patriotic and proud of their male relatives who were joining the forces. Young women in particular really wanted to be part of the war effort, often seeing it not just as a patriotic duty but as an opportunity to escape from the confines of the family home. The combination of romance and usefulness of being a nurse in wartime meant no shortage of volunteers for the Voluntary Aid Detachments, set up across Britain to care for people injured in the bombing, or the First Aid Nursing Yeomanry (FANY), which despite its name carried out a number of other roles apart from nursing, including providing drivers for Bletchley Park. Women also became ambulance drivers, worked in factories, on farms, or joined the fire service or the police. Female equivalents of the Royal Navy, the Army and the Royal Air Force had all been set up during the First World War but then disbanded in the early 1920s. In the run-up to war, they were re-formed. The Women's Royal Naval Service, commonly known as the Wrens, the Women's Auxiliary Air Force or WAAF, and the female equivalent of the Army, the Auxiliary Territorial Service or ATS, became the most common organisations in which young women sought to serve their country, along with the weapons factories and 'the Land Army' of female farm workers.

Despite all this patriotic enthusiasm, recruitment of extra staff for Bletchley was initially slow. There was very little money available, and that was likely to remain the case unless the codebreakers could find a way into the German Enigma codes and begin to prove their worth, but morale remained remarkably high. As Christmas approached, Phoebe naturally wanted to spend it at home with her mother, but someone had to stay behind and keep track of the German messages.

'It was impossible for us all to be away together so we arranged among ourselves who should stay. Jocelyn and I drew lots and I lost and resigned myself to a miserable Christmas, the first one for some years that I had spent away from home. When the day arrived I found there were more people at BP than I had thought there would be.'

There was a ban on travel over the Christmas period so even some of those who had got time off couldn't get home. Frank Birch invited Phoebe and the other members of the German Naval Section who were on duty for drinks in the office.

'I arrived afterwards in the dining room for lunch feeling quite happy and, being rather late, to find the hall decorated magnificently with everyone sitting down wearing the peculiar paper hats one gets from Christmas crackers and blowing whistles which shot out a terrific length of paper. Every seat was occupied with the exception of one seat round the corner but there I sat quite happily with a wonderful lunch in front of me. All the Christmases which I spent in Bletchley were extremely good, everyone going all out to make everyone else enjoy themselves.'

By now Dilly Knox and Alan Turing, working in the Cottage, had begun to realise there was something wrong with the information the Poles had given them on the Enigma machine. Fortunately, the Polish mathematicians had escaped ahead of the advancing German troops and were now in France. Early in the New Year, Mr Turing went to visit them at the chateau east of Paris where the French codebreaking organisation was based to collect the correct information from the Poles. Shortly after Turing came back, Dilly broke into the German Army's main administrative Enigma code. A few weeks later, he managed to solve the main operational Enigma code of the Luftwaffe, the German Air Force.

One of the newly recruited mathematicians who had been sent to work on Enigma with Dilly Knox was Gordon Welchman, a 33-year-old mathematics lecturer at Sidney Sussex College, Cambridge. He'd realised very quickly that once Enigma was broken they would need a very efficient system to decode the German messages, produce intelligence reports on what the messages said, and then pass that intelligence on to the commanders who could make use of it as quickly as possible.

Mr Welchman, a studious, pipe-smoking man who was far more dynamic than his academic appearance suggested, decided they would need two sections right next to each other: one full of codebreakers breaking the German messages and the other full of intelligence officers writing the reports for the generals and Whitehall.

Even before his idea was backed by his bosses, Mr Welchman had begun recruiting his own people to man the codebreaking section, which was to be based in the newly built Hut 6 and would deal with the German army and air force Enigma codes. Welchman's codebreaking section would be known only as Hut 6, for security reasons. No one was to know they were breaking Enigma.

Stuart Milner-Barry, the 33-year-old chess correspondent of *The Times* and formerly a fellow undergraduate of Gordon Welchman's at Trinity College, Cambridge, was one of the first to join Hut 6 as Mr Welchman's deputy. When the war broke out he had been in Argentina playing chess for Britain, along with his friends, Hugh Alexander and Harry Golombek. They too soon agreed to join Mr Milner-Barry, as did the Scottish chess champion J.M. 'Max' Aitken and another mathematician, Dennis Babbage from Magdalene College, Cambridge. The sort of men and women who could think through a chess puzzle were soon seen as precisely the right people to work out how to break a complex enemy code.

In the meantime, it was the people working on the lower-level codes in the naval, air and military sections who were producing the main intelligence coming out of Bletchley. Phoebe, Jocelyn Bostock and Doreen Henderson, who had become known as Susie, were gathering important intelligence for the Royal Navy from what was called 'traffic analysis', just reading the transcripts from the Navy's wireless intercept sites at Scarborough and Winchester and working out what the German ships and submarines (U-boats) were doing from that.

Something similar was going on in the Air Section at the other end of Hut 4, where they were breaking low-level Luftwaffe codes and analysing the radio networks to gather intelligence which was passed direct to the Air Ministry in London – for the first couple of years of the war, however, the ministry seemed to ignore anything Bletchley said. The section was headed by Josh Cooper, who had joined the Code and Cypher School in the 1920s and was a very experienced codebreaker, but he was also regarded as slightly eccentric by some of the new recruits.

His personal assistant Ann Lavell, an eighteen-year-old WAAF, thought he was permanently distracted because there was so much going on in his mind. On one occasion, standing looking at the ducks on the lake, while eating a sandwich with one hand and holding a mug of coffee in the other, Mr Cooper finished most of the sandwich and, although presumably intending to feed the rest of it to the ducks, threw the mug not the sandwich into the lake. It was the sort of behaviour, common among some of the older codebreakers and newly employed university professors, which made the younger recruits think that people like Josh Cooper were, in Ann's words, 'absolutely mad'.

'When I got to know him I got quite fond of him. But he was not really one of us. He was on another plane, I think. He'd get awfully embarrassed and worried when he felt he wasn't acting like an ordinary human being. There was one time when he kicked over a fire extinguisher and it started foaming and he didn't know what to do and he picked it up, rushed to and fro, and a friend of mine went and took it from him and put it out of the window. He wasn't very practical but once you knew him and got over the slightly forbidding exterior he was very nice and very kind. I've got a rather delightful caricature of him, doing this very familiar gesture of right hand behind head and scratching his left ear.'

The impression that all these strange intellectuals were rather eccentric took hold. When Gwen Davies was sent to Bletchley Park as an eighteen-year-old member of the WAAF, she was told initially that she was being posted to nearby RAF Chicksands. 'When I arrived at Chicksands I was taken into the administration office where there was a driver waiting and he said with perfect seriousness: "Do we blindfold her or do we use the covered van?" and ultimately they used the covered van. I was shut into the back of a blacked-out van and taken to Bletchley.'

She was dumped with her luggage outside the gates of the Park and told by a young guard that she couldn't come in because she didn't have a pass. 'I was by this time hungry, thirsty and very, very annoyed. "Look," I said, "I don't know where I am, and I don't know what I'm supposed to do." "Come to the right place then," said the guard, "most of 'em here look as if they didn't know where they was and God knows what they'm doing."

'An elderly guard told him to leave me alone, and said that I was to go to the hut at the left of the gates. "Somebody will come and see to you," he said, "and if you want to know where you are, you're at Bletchley Park." "And if you want to know what that is," added the younger guard, sniggering, "it's the biggest lunatic asylum in Britain."'

2

Breaking Enigma

Jane Hughes told all her friends she was lucky to get out of St Moritz with her virginity intact. It was the late summer of 1938. Jane was still only seventeen. She'd spent an idyllic year at Sadler's Wells, training to be a ballet dancer, sharing the studios with a new, up-and-coming young dancer called Margot Fonteyn. But just as Jane's career seemed to be taking off, Ninette de Valois, the head of the school, hit her on the back with a stick during class.

'That back's too long and you're too tall. I'm afraid we can't use you.'

Jane, who'd given up everything to be a ballet dancer, was distraught. So, to help her get over it, her parents sent her and a friend to spend six months learning German with a highly respectable doctor in the dull Zurich suburb of Rüschlikon. Not long after arriving there, Jane saw a poster of skiers on the snow-covered Alps at St Moritz at the city's railway station.

'So I immediately rang up my parents and said: "We're

off to St Moritz." What was the point of being down in Rüschlikon when we could be up there?'

They replaced the respectable doctor from Rüschlikon with a new, more interesting doctor in St Moritz who was very happy to take in young lady lodgers and teach them German. It turned out to be a far more educational experience than Jane's parents had planned.

'I didn't really understand what was happening, of course, but he kept snuggling closer and closer to me on the sofa and I just thought he was feeling rather cold or something. Not a bit of it. Apparently, he was a well-known womaniser. Anyway, we still went on learning German. Probably learned it better up there than we did down in Rüschlikon . . . Then came the dreaded season.'

Jane's mother called her back to London, insisting it was now time for her to 'come out'. After leaving school, young women of a certain class, known as debutantes, would spend the summer months in a whirl of cocktail and champagne 'coming-out' parties, dances and social events like Ascot and Wimbledon at which they would be introduced to young men who were deemed to be suitable husbands. The 'season', as it was known, would begin with all of the 'Debs' being presented to the Queen at court. Jane regarded it as a complete waste of both her parents' money and her precious time. Given the limits of a tan acquired on the ski slopes, she was also deeply embarrassed at being forced to wear a strapless gown.

'My face was very, very dark brown because I'd been in the sun for so long but my shoulders were absolutely white, so it was the most ludicrous sight and I cried and cried when I was put into this ridiculous outfit and told I'd got to go off to my first dance.'

Jane wasn't alone in hating the whole thing and it seemed to her that, while some of the girls clearly enjoyed the partying, the people who got the most fun out of it all were the mothers, competing with each other to host the best parties and secure the most promising husbands for their daughters.

'Most of the girls were rather resentful at being made to waste some of their lifeblood on it. There were lots of very vapid boys who were called "Debs' Delights", who tried to lure everybody under the staircases. They didn't get too far because you had to be chaperoned everywhere you went, so you had your mother or somebody else sitting around. There was always somebody on watch.'

Then out of the blue, a letter arrived from Elizabeth Blandy, one of Jane's closest friends from Miss Ironside's, the high-class Kensington school for young ladies which, while providing them both with a good education, had taken a rather sniffy view of the usefulness to a girl's future of exams or university.

'Elizabeth's father was in wine and bananas in Madeira, rather a wealthy man. She was at this curious little school with me in South Kensington so I'd known her all my life.'

It was February 1940, just a few weeks after Dilly Knox had made the first breaks into the Enigma codes. Elizabeth had been recruited to work in the newly created Hut 6 where those first successes against Enigma suddenly meant there was a great deal of work to do. But recruitment for Bletchley was still very slow, hamstrung by the fact that so few people knew they were breaking the German codes, by the armed forces having the pick of all the brightest young men, and by the continuing belief that only a certain type of person could be trusted to keep the secret. Elizabeth had been recommended by friends of her father and now, like all the young women in Hut 6, she was asked if she knew anyone else who might be available and able to keep a secret. Naturally, she turned to Jane.

'Elizabeth wrote and said: "Well, Jane. I'm at Bletchley and it's perfectly frightful. We're so overworked, so desperately busy. You must come and join us." She invited me to come to lunch.'

Despite the unpromising tone of the letter, Jane accepted the invitation and, after lunch in the mansion, was taken into Hut 6 and interviewed by Stuart Milner-Barry, who'd only arrived a couple of weeks earlier himself. Jane was still only eighteen. She was impressed to find Mr Milner-Barry working there because she knew he was rather a famous chess player, but wasn't quite so impressed by his confidence around women.

'I don't think he'd ever given an interview in his life, certainly not to a young girl. Desperately shy. He couldn't think of a single thing to say and I couldn't think of anything to say to him because I wasn't supposed to say anything.'

After five minutes of silence interspersed with Mr Milner-Barry's efforts to work out whether Jane was suitable, he told her he was taking her to see 'the boss', Commander Edward Travis, the deputy head of Bletchley Park, who had just as much difficulty talking to her, albeit for slightly different reasons.

'He started trying to tell me about what was happening there, but of course they couldn't say anything. But he did say that there was an important job to be done and that everybody ought to do it if they were able to because it was so vital.'

By now, Jane had decided that, despite Elizabeth's gloomy letter and the uninformative interviews with the Bletchley bosses, there was clearly an interesting job to be done and she had no doubt that she was the right sort of person to do it. She signed the Official Secrets Act and agreed to report for work the following Monday.

'I went off home and told my parents: "I've joined the Foreign Office." They were rather amazed and said: "Well, where are you going?" I said Buckinghamshire, which they didn't find very convincing. Anyway, I packed up my bags and turned up on Monday morning at the gate, had a bit of trouble with the sentries, and eventually got in.'

She was told that the Germans were using a complex machine called Enigma to encode their messages. The settings for the machine, which were also known as the keys, changed every day and Hut 6 was trying to break the German army and air force versions. There were a number of wireless stations around the UK intercepting the German messages. The operators at these stations wrote down the messages on pre-printed forms. These were then rushed by motorcycle courier to Bletchley, to Hut 6.

There were only thirty people working in Hut 6 when Jane arrived. Most of the rooms were almost entirely manned by young male mathematics graduates recruited from Cambridge and a few other universities deemed to be producing good mathematicians. Only the room where Jane was to work was completely staffed by women.

The hut itself was made up of four main sections, the first being the Registration Room: here messages were sorted into types, the key elements like the wireless frequency it was sent on were noted down and attempts made to work out which units were part of the various radio networks that were being intercepted. They were looking for any information that might help crack the code.

The Intercept Control Room talked to the intercept stations to make sure they were taking the messages that would be the best ones to break and that each German network was being intercepted by the station which could hear it most clearly. It was absolutely vital that the intercept operators got every letter right.

The main codebreaking took place in the Machine Room, so-called because the young mathematicians working there had a real Enigma machine which they could use to test out their theories of what the day's settings for each code might be.

The Germans were using a number of different types of Enigma code, with each part of the *Wehrmacht*, the German armed forces, using their own system. The different Enigma codes were identified in Hut 6 by colours because they used different-coloured crayons to record their progress against each Enigma system on paper charts pinned to the wall.

Once the codebreakers in the Machine Room had broken the daily settings for one type of Enigma, they moved on to another. They didn't decode the messages. That was done by the young women in the Decoding Room where Jane and Elizabeth worked.

The Decoding Room didn't have any real Enigma machines. They had British cipher machines, called Typex, which had been converted to work in the same way as an Enigma machine. When the mathematicians had broken the day's keys for one of the Enigma codes, they passed them on to Jane or one of the other girls in the Decoding Room. They then set up their machines using those keys and typed up all the messages encoded using that particular system.

But while Jane and the others were happy to work extremely hard to try to help win the war, they suffered from very poor working conditions which weren't helped by the smoky atmosphere in the hut. It seemed almost obligatory for the young mathematicians to smoke a pipe while they were working out their puzzles, and the ventilation was very poor. Jane wasn't used to these types of conditions at all.

'It was very bad accommodation. Very cold in the winter and very hot in the summer. No insulation of any kind except for blackout curtains. We had horrid little trestle tables, which were very wobbly, and collapsible chairs, which were also very wobbly, very hard. There was very poor lighting; single light bulbs hanging down from the ceiling. So we were really in semi-darkness, which I expect is what the authorities wanted, better security.'

The converted Typex machines fed out decoded messages in lines of text on strips of paper tape, like the tape used for old-fashioned telegrams. The girls had to check that it was in German and then glue the paper tape with the decoded message onto the back of the original message.

When Diana Russell-Clarke first arrived at Bletchley she was still in the Naval Section and had started out in the library working on Italian messages, but because Hut 6 was desperate for women who spoke German to work in the Decoding Room, she was transferred over to there. Diana had been taught by a German governess so she could tell if the settings worked out by the mathematicians were working and the messages were coming out in German.

'But a lot of it was not particularly clear because of course it gets rather jumbled up coming over the air, but one knew quite a lot of what it was. Of course, a lot of the stuff was very routine, orders to people in the Luftwaffe and things, but occasionally you got this great excitement.'

The messages, still in German, were put into a cardboard box and pushed through a makeshift wooden tunnel with a broom handle into Hut 3 next door where they were turned into intelligence reports and sent to London.

Given the difficulties finding enough good young mathematicians, and the success in recruiting more women for the Decoding Room, Mr Milner-Barry decided to staff the Registration Room with women as well. The young male mathematicians could then all be put in the Machine Room to concentrate on the actual codebreaking. He went back to Cambridge, to the women's colleges of Girton and Newnham, where his sister had been vice-principal, to recruit a number of young female graduates.

Joy Higgins was twenty-one and studying English Literature at Cambridge. Her father was the headmaster of a school in Newport Pagnell, about eight miles north of Bletchley Park, so an invitation to work there was attractive. She'd already visited the mansion before the war, when the estate was put up for sale. The contents of the house were being auctioned off and her mother wanted to buy some of the high-quality porcelain and glassware.

'Now the Park was surrounded by a high perimeter fence, with a military guard at the entrance gates. I was to report to a small hut outside these gates, and it was here that I was interviewed by Frank Birch, a recalled First World War expert, and Harold Fletcher, who had been a distinguished Cambridge mathematician. Unorthodox as ever, the former was wearing a pea-green shirt and a Breton beret.'

Mr Fletcher, who was dressed more conservatively, was in charge of all the Hut 6 sections that were now to be staffed by women. Joy thought him charming. He and Mr Birch asked her a lot of odd questions and gave her a piece of Italian text to translate which she stumbled through somehow. When they asked her if she expected to get a First, she crossed her fingers and said she hoped so.

'They couldn't tell me what the work involved because of its secret nature, but they thought I was a suitable candidate, and soon afterwards a letter arrived at home inviting me to work at Bletchley Park as a technical assistant, once I came down from Cambridge.'

On the Monday after Joy finished her degree, she arrived at Bletchley, signed the Official Secrets Act, was given a pass and told she'd be paid £195 a year plus ten shillings (50p) a week war bonus. She was then taken into the Registration Room, which was already full of young female graduates, mostly from Cambridge, but some from Oxford and Aberdeen.

'It was a good place to start as it began to give a general picture of what happened in Hut 6, and an overall idea of the work of Bletchley Park as a whole. People did go to immense lengths to explain things to us, always within the strict bounds of security. The questions of my interview made sense now. Certainly they needed the trained minds and the discipline of the graduate; but they also needed an attention to detail, a sense of order – and much enthusiasm.'

Each of the women working in the Registration Room was allocated to one specific Enigma system. The lists of messages they compiled were known as B-Lists, so the new female intake swiftly became known as the 'Blisters'. The German messages were sent using Morse code in groups of five letters but at the beginning of the message the operator sent a number of things like time of origin and the settings. This was called 'the preamble' and was the part of the message they had to concentrate on.

Pamela Draughn, another 21-year-old, had been study-ing French and German at Royal Holloway College when she was recruited to be a Blister.

'All the time I was at college I was always discouraged from going into the forces. I wasn't frightfully keen to but I just wanted to be doing something useful and Old French and Middle-High German, I used to think, was the most useless thing I could be doing.'

So she applied to the Foreign Office for a job, thinking

she would be travelling the world, and after successfully passing the interviews was told to report to London from where she and another young female recruit were driven to Bletchley Park. They were met by Mr Fletcher, who told them what they would be doing and, as part of a long lecture on the need for complete secrecy, informed them that they were now banned from leaving the country for the duration of the war. They couldn't risk anyone being captured by the Germans and giving the secret away. It was not quite what Pam wanted to hear, but she bit her lip and got on with it. Fletcher sent her to join Joy in the Registration Room.

'You had a sheet which was called a B-List on which you analysed each message which came in which was believed to be in your code. You put down the number of letters, the origin and the frequency. Occasionally there was a third group of letters used.'

One of the most important things Pam had to note down was the number of groups in each message.

'If you saw exactly the same-length message sent out at the same time you could think that it might be a re-encodement from one code into another and that would help enormously because if you'd broken one code you could break the other code.'

During the early spring of 1940, Hut 6 stopped being able to break Enigma. The main code they'd been working on was a Luftwaffe system which allowed the German Air Force to talk to the two other services. The codebreakers called this the Red and used red crayons to chart their progress against it. It was already clear from the time when they had been breaking it that if only they could decode it, there was a lot of intelligence to be had, but they just couldn't get back into it. When the Germans invaded Denmark and Norway in April they used a completely different Enigma code, which Hut 6 called Yellow. It was much easier to break than the Red and produced lots of details of German operations and plans, but there was very little that could be done with the intelligence. British troops could do nothing to stop the Germans invading Norway and the ineffectual response led in early May to Mr Chamberlain's resignation as Prime Minister and his replacement by Winston Churchill. The new Prime Minister told Parliament that he had nothing to offer the British people 'but blood, toil, tears and sweat' and that they had no choice but to win the war. The nation's very survival depended on it.

There might not have been much blood spilled at Bletchley, but there was certainly toil, sweat and tears. The invasions of Norway and Denmark, and the certain knowledge that Holland, Belgium and France would be next, forced Hut 6 to work round the clock, with two or three people working in each room overnight. But plans to put the Blisters and the Decoders on night shifts alongside the men were blocked by senior civil servants worried about what young men and women working together through the night would get up to.

The bosses wanted to put three women on the Hut 6 night shift, since this was all that was needed to keep the B-Lists up to date and do the decoding. The Civil

Service bosses insisted there must be six women on shift. Mr Milner-Barry said sarcastically that this was probably because the men would be 'overworked' trying to keep so many women happy. Three women had to be brought in from another hut to sit on the night shift doing nothing in order to protect the other three girls' morals. Given the shortage of staff across the Park, this stupidity was dispensed with after a couple of weeks.

Most of the women were in billets with people they'd never met before, some of whom were welcoming, some of whom were definitely not. They had to pay their own rent, which was set at a guinea a week. Joy Higgins was lucky.

'I explained that I could live at home and every week I religiously paid my mother the statutory one guinea for my board and lodging.'

Others weren't so fortunate, although most eventually found somewhere reasonable to stay. Ailsa Macdonald was reading economics at Edinburgh when she was recruited. She and two other girls were placed in a house in Wolverton, where a large number of the young women were billeted. It was a pretty disastrous couple of months.

'We shared a small bedroom, three of us. They had a bathroom but we weren't allowed to use it. After quite a short time we were moved. I was sent to a new housing estate and it was a modern house. They had a small child and I was very happy there. But I was lucky because I think a lot of people had billets where the sanitary facilities were not very good.'

Jane was billeted in a lorry driver's house right in the

middle of Bletchley itself. He drove for the London Brick Company and their works were just behind the house. They were overshadowed by large brick chimneys 'belching out horrible raucous smoke', one of which towered right above them. 'It really was disgusting.' The town itself was a major railway junction and the fast trains to and from Scotland shook the whole house. The lorry driver and his wife were kind and hospitable but with Jane frequently working night shifts, she found it impossible to sleep.

'The room they gave me was a cupboard really with a tiny window. They had two little boys who were quite noisy and I, of course, was on the night shift a lot of the time. So I couldn't really sleep when the boys were at home and it was about as uncomfortable a place as I've ever slept in.'

As the work in Hut 6 built up, Jane found herself increasingly tired and soon became very run-down. Her father was very worried about her and eventually one of his friends, Sir Reginald Bonsor, said his country home wasn't that far from Bletchley. Most of the servants had been called up so they had plenty of spare rooms. Why didn't Jane come and stay with them?

'I was transferred to this very grandiose Elizabethan house and they happened to have rather a lot of rooms empty because they had lost pretty much the whole of their staff. So I was able to move in about half a dozen of my friends, and that became much more jolly, of course.'

The mansion was at Liscombe Park, eight miles south of Bletchley. Jane and her friends, along with all the other people living in billets, were taken into Bletchley at the start of each shift by buses or large estate cars, known as shooting brakes, which were driven by members of the FANY, or the Motor Transport Corps, a volunteer organisation made up of young women. Barbara Abernethy's ability to organise the early entertainment like the rounders matches had been spotted and she'd been moved from the Naval Section into administration, coordinating things like transport.

'The Motor Transport Corps drivers were really very attractive girls. They were usually quite wealthy and they had to buy their own uniforms, which were beautifully cut, and they were all very pretty. But they worked very, very hard.'

The only problem with living in a country mansion for Jane and her friends was that when they were going on the night shift they had to wend their way along a dark drive and even darker country lanes shrouded in high hedges and trees to get to the transport pick-up point.

'So one had to get to the right place and be confident that the driver had been told by the previous driver exactly where they were to pick you up. We felt a bit vulnerable and I was accused of taking a hammer with me, although actually it was a torch which was far more useful.'

They then did the rounds of surrounding villages picking up other people in various houses, cottages and pubs, which took a considerable time and cut into the amount of time they had off.

'But otherwise it was a wonderful place to live. We had lovely rooms, of course, and very beautiful gardens, and one was able to relax in a quite different extent to being in the heart of Bletchley.'

Occasionally, Lady Bonsor invited them down for proper

dinner parties. Pretty young women were always welcome when young officers back from the war were being feted.

'That was quite a do, because they had a cook left behind when all the others were called up, so they had very good food and we really enjoyed ourselves. Very unlike a lot of people who were in rather horrible billets.'

The invasion of France in May 1940 was to bring a swift victory for the Germans and a humiliating defeat for the French and British forces, but it provided Bletchley with a major success that would help win many more battles in the future. As the Germans swept through Holland, Belgium and into France, they sent more than a thousand Enigma messages a day and at times the entire hut was overwhelmed, with many of the staff, including the young women in the Registration and Decoding Rooms, working nonstop and not going home. Diana remembered snatching a few precious moments' sleep on the floor of the Decoding Room.

'There was a time when we were working certainly forty-eight hours on end because there was a lot of traffic coming through and they hadn't really got enough staff and the stuff perhaps would stop for a bit and we just used to put our coats under our head and lie on the floor and go to sleep.'

But the large number of messages being sent by the Germans helped the bright young codebreakers in the Machine Room break back into the Red, in large part due to some extremely clever thinking by John Herivel, one of the Cambridge mathematicians. He put himself into the mind of a German Enigma operator and worked out a mistake that tired operators might make. Ten days into the battle, several operators all made that very same mistake and Hut 6 was back into the Red Enigma, guaranteeing that they would produce good intelligence for the rest of the war. Everyone in the Machine Room was cheering and shouting and the elation was felt throughout the hut.

MI6 sent communication experts and intelligence officers out to France to pass on the codebreakers' reports to the British commanders but the Allied forces were overwhelmed and it had little effect. The British troops had to be evacuated from Dunkirk by several dozen Royal Navy ships and a volunteer armada of small boats from England's southern ports which helped to lift the soldiers off the beaches. Just as the codebreakers had listened in the mansion to Mr Chamberlain telling them on the BBC they were at war with Germany, so in June 1940 they listened to Mr Churchill saying that they would 'ride out the storm of war, and outlive the menace of tyranny, if necessary for years, if necessary alone'.

It was stirring stuff. Britain would never surrender, the Prime Minister said. 'We shall defend our Island, whatever the cost may be. We shall fight on the beaches and on the landing grounds. We shall fight in the fields and in the streets. We shall fight in the hills.' The staff at Bletchley listened and, despite their worries, they were proud. They knew Britain was now alone, but they also knew that they had the opportunity, a unique opportunity, to help to win the war.

Britain collectively waited for what seemed the inevitable German invasion. Bletchley Park set up its own rather odd-ball 'Dad's Army' Home Guard detachment, with Alan Turing as one of the unlikely defenders, and plans were made to set up a mobile codebreaking team that would be evacuated if the Germans invaded to keep breaking the codes and provide the vital intelligence. Phoebe Senyard was bemused by the reaction of some of the codebreakers.

'The war situation was now becoming very grim for us. The air was electric with feeling. Those who had been chosen were in a sense excited by the prospect before them, although no doubt dismayed by the reason for their evacuation. I was surprised by the number of people whose feelings were hurt because they had not been included on the list.'

In another rousing speech, Mr Churchill told the nation that while the Battle for France had been lost, the Battle of Britain was about to begin. They should brace themselves to do their duty so that if Britain, its Empire and its Commonwealth were to last for a thousand years, men would still say: 'This was their finest hour.'

The Germans attempted to intimidate Britain ahead of Hitler's planned invasion, Operation Sea Lion, testing the ability of the RAF to defend the skies above southern England. RAF Hurricanes and Spitfires circled the skies, taking on the German Messerschmitt fighters in Mr Churchill's Battle of Britain. When that failed, Hitler launched a campaign of mass intimidation, the Blitz, the bombing of Britain's cities and ports. This was the moment that Hut 6 had its first major impact on the war. They broke the Enigma code used by the Luftwaffe to direct its bombers to their targets. The wireless network which used what Hut 6 called the Brown Enigma controlled the radio beams that guided the German pilots to their targets and, around midday every day, it named the targets for that night's raids. The codebreakers sent the targets straight to London so that RAF fighter aircraft could be sent up to wait in ambush for the German bombers and the authorities in the cities concerned could start making preparations. A number of 'safe' cities were always warned as well as the real targets, to protect the Enigma secret. The breaking of the Brown Enigma meant the air defences were ready. It substantially reduced the damage done on the ground, saving factories that were producing goods vital to the war effort. But just as importantly, it saved many lives. The authorities were able to get people safely down into the air-raid shelters before the German bombers arrived.

No one in Hut 6 was in any doubt as to how important their work was. Those who lived in the big cities had been home and seen how many people's houses had been turned to rubble, knew people who had lost loved ones. Some had even lost close relatives themselves in the bombing. Even if you didn't live in a big city, you would see the impact of the bombing on your days off when you visited London. But, like all the Enigma codes, there were days when the Brown Enigma simply couldn't be broken. In November 1940, for four straight days, Hut 6 failed to unravel it. One of those days was 14 November. Diana came on shift at four o'clock that afternoon.

'It was a day when they hadn't broken the code. Quite late in the day, sometime in the evening, all these German bombers started streaming over so we knew someone was being blown up and we hadn't been able to alert them.'

The German bombers were heading for Coventry, which lay undefended by RAF fighter aircraft. The raid destroyed large parts of the city, including the cathedral, and killed 600 people. A myth grew up that Bletchley had known the raid was going to take place and that Coventry was the target, but that the Prime Minister ordered them not to say anything to prevent the Germans realising that British Intelligence had decoded the supposedly unbreakable Enigma code. It wasn't true. Why if it were would he have allowed them to warn other cities like Birmingham, or Manchester, or Cardiff, or Liverpool, that they were going to be attacked? But the accusation stuck, unfairly tainting the reputations of both Mr Churchill and Bletchley.

The codebreakers' ability to crack Enigma dramatically improved in late 1940 when a new machine designed by Alan Turing and Gordon Welchman was installed in the Park. The Bombe was based on an idea by the Poles, who before the war had linked several Enigma machines together to try to test out possible settings faster than you could by using just one machine. The Poles had called their machine the *Bomba*, or bomb, because it made a ticking noise like a time bomb.

The British machine was much larger and noisier than that. It was a huge electro-mechanical machine set in a bronze cabinet six and a half feet high, more than seven feet wide and two and a half feet deep. It contained a series of thirty rotating drums, designed to replicate the action of ten Enigma machines. The codebreakers in the

Machine Room tried to break the code using a stream of plain German text, known as a 'crib', which they believed was hidden somewhere in the encoded message. Once they had worked out where they thought it was, they created a program for the Bombe. It was known as a 'menu' and linked the encoded letters and the letters of the German together. This menu was given to the Bombe operators who set up the machine according to the menu. The Bombe then ran through all the possible options much faster than a human being could have done and helped to speed up the codebreaking process. The first Bombe that worked properly was introduced in August 1940. It was given the name *Agnus Dei* (Lamb of God) but was swiftly nicknamed Agnes, or Aggie for short.

There wasn't much time off for anyone in Hut 6 but a Bletchley Park Recreational Club was set up with a small library, a drama group, musical and choral societies as well as bridge, chess, fencing and Scottish dancing sections. Jane and Diana joined the choral society. Jane's father had been an accomplished singer, who had performed with Vaughan Williams, and she was something of a singer herself.

'We gave concerts, of course, the usual kind of thing. I wouldn't say it was a very high standard of music that we put out. I remember us inspiring each other because it was so wonderful to sing.'

She and Diana also joined the Scottish dance group organised by Hugh Foss, one of the pre-war codebreakers, who was an established authority on Scottish country dancing and famous back in Scotland for having devised a number of new dances. Before the war, he had helped run the Chelsea Reel Society of which Commander Denniston had been another of the leading members. Jane thought Mr Foss was delightfully eccentric.

'He had wonderful brogues that were knitted all the way up the front of his legs. He was very tall and certainly looked very eccentric, but he was a very good reel dancer. I suppose he'd spent his whole life at it and he was very keen to get more and more members so it became quite big. We all attended regularly because we all enjoyed it.'

There were very occasional weeks of leave but in the early days these were few and far between. Nevertheless, it was possible to save up days off and between a run of night shifts and a run of evening shifts they could come off the night shift first thing in the morning of one day. The following day would be their day off and they would then come back on shift on the evening of the next day, effectively giving them more than two days off. Most of Pam's family were back home in Scotland but her father was working in London.

'I would save up my days together and go and see him, or save up more time and go up to Scotland to see the rest of the family. So I wasn't very often in the billets, except just to feed and to sleep. I was quite fortunate that my father worked for the London, Midland and Scottish Railway so I had free travel.'

Jane and her friends sometimes took the train but often hitchhiked down Watling Street into London and, when her boyfriend Ted, an officer in the Royal Navy, was not at sea, she would leave her friends and make a beeline for the HMV record store in Oxford Street to meet up with him.

'They had these wonderful little listening capsules with two little seats and you turned on your favourite Mozart and just sat there in complete privacy for as long as you wanted. So we had the most wonderful time in HMV, listening to a lot of beautiful music and having a few precious moments together. But of course, all too soon we had to hitch a lift from a lorry back to Bletchley.'

Mair Thomas, from Pontycymer in the Welsh valleys, was at Cardiff University studying music when she was recruited to work at Bletchley in a scene that could have come from a spy novel. She was sat in the university library when a man tapped her on the shoulder. He had a posh English accent and told her he was from the Foreign Office. Somehow, he'd heard she was good at languages and liked solving puzzles. They needed people like her for hush-hush work. So she'd have to be able to keep a secret.

'He was the classic tall, dark stranger. It sounded important, serious, and if I'm honest, a little bit glamorous. He said I'd be solving problems and using my language skills for the country. I should write to the Foreign Office in Whitehall and express my interest. With that, he turned and left.'

Mair wrote to the Foreign Office describing the encounter with the tall, dark stranger and saying that she wanted to apply for the post he'd mentioned, even though she'd no idea at all what the post was. She was called up to London, to the Foreign Office, where she was interviewed and told the bare bones of the job, including the fact that it involved breaking the German codes, before being made to sign the Official Secrets Act. She arrived in Hut 6 in August 1941, aged twenty-three, and despite having just spent a couple of years at university was struck by the informality of the place.

'There were people scurrying around busily, some in uniform, although most were dressed in civilian clothes. This also varied enormously. I saw men in dark suits, but I also saw quite a few in jumpers and even corduroy trousers. The women were on the whole smartly dressed in frocks and jackets, but many of them wore colourful stockings. Every day witnessed an array of colourful and sometimes gaudy leg adornments and they served to raise spirits in an intense and generally serious atmosphere.'

A few weeks after she arrived, Mr Churchill visited the Park, standing on a pile of rubble to address those who were working, thanking them for all their hard work and ending by telling them that they were 'the geese who laid the golden egg but never cackled'. The applause was deafening. He toured Hut 6 and stood behind Mair, saying that it must be very difficult to use the big, clunky Typex machine.

'My mind turned to soup; I couldn't think of anything to say. I may even have curtseyed out of embarrassment. Thankfully, Mr Welchman could see I was struggling and explained to him the complexity of the German Enigma and how they changed their code settings every day. On their way out Mr Welchman touched my arm and told me not to worry, that all of us were feeling nervous with the PM about.'

Mair found her new colleagues friendly, but as a devout Christian there was one aspect of life in the Park which Mair didn't like at all. Women of that era were brought up very strictly and were often fairly innocent, even ignorant, of sexual matters. But the dangers and uncertainties of war, the freedom of being away from home, and the mix of so many young men and women together, inevitably led some to live for the day.

'Quite honestly people's morals were very loose; men and women swapping partners all the time, it seemed to me. Quite a number of the men were married, but this didn't stop them forming secret relationships. This was one of the dark sides of Bletchley.'

Many of the women in Hut 6 had boyfriends in the forces and were not interested in the male codebreakers, but Diana was free and single and determined to make the most of it.

'We all had a marvellous time, all these young men, not attached. We had a very gay time going out to pubs for supper together when we were free. A lot of romance went on, very definitely a lot of romance. The whole thing was absolutely tremendous fun. It's rather awful in the middle of the war. We had to be there, it was an emergency and I think we all put our hearts into it. But I think we all enjoyed being there.'

Diana was particularly taken by one man. She wasn't the only one to regard Dennis Babbage, one of the brightest of the mathematicians, as a bit of a catch. Although Jane was in love with her naval officer and not interested in other men, she too thought Mr Babbage rather good-looking.

Diana was very keen on him and it was not long before they were married. But it was soon clear that it was a disaster.

'Babbage was a very attractive man but we had no sexual intercourse on the whole of our honeymoon so I could just have had the thing annulled but of course I didn't. He was a charming person.'

There was something of a minor scandal when shortly after they arrived back at Bletchley, moving into a house together in Woburn Sands, one of Diana's friends began pursuing Mr Babbage. Jane was unaware of the problems on the honeymoon and was quite shocked by the speed at which it all happened.

'This girl pinched him from his very new wife. He was only married a while before he got into her clutches. It might have been a few weeks. It felt like a very short time. Dennis was a great scholar but he was rather good-looking, that was probably one of the reasons that he got snapped up so quickly.'

Diana took it in her stride, remaining friends with Dennis and going on to marry the slightly older Geoffrey Barraclough, a renowned medieval historian, who was working as a senior intelligence officer in Hut 3. But another love tangle was to have far more serious effects.

One of the girls in Hut 6, Mary, a young Glaswegian woman, had been dating someone in Hut 8 (the naval Enigma section), but he had also been seeing a lot of Gillian, another of the Hut 6 girls. The rivalry exploded in the canteen, where the boring if filling nature of the food ensured that all the attention was on the row between the two young women.

Mary was particularly upset at what she clearly saw as a threat to her own relationship with the Hut 8 codebreaker and told Gillian that he'd shared lots of secrets about codes that had been broken and gave some examples in an attempt to try to demonstrate that it was her he was really keen on. Gillian's response, claiming that he had passed on other even more important secrets to her, and naming some of them, only escalated the row.

Mair was sat at the same table watching and listening in horror. She liked both girls although she'd been worried before by their willingness to chat about work in a way which they'd been told never to do. But this was far worse than anything they'd done before.

'Everyone froze and went silent. Both girls realised that they had taken this too far and I looked around the crowded canteen to see if anyone was coming to tell them off. After a few moments, Mary looked as if she was going to reply but I piped up and told them both not to say any more or they would be in serious trouble. We all dispersed and made our way back to the hut.'

But that wasn't the end of it. No sooner had they got back into Hut 6 than they started all over again, each claiming more secrets that the other girl hadn't been told. Suddenly, one of the female supervisors stormed into the room. She'd received a complaint from someone who'd heard the row in the canteen.

'I cannot believe what I've just heard,' she said. 'Or the gossip you indulged in during lunch. You have signed the Official Secrets Act. You have said things that should never have been said or repeated and you've disgraced yourselves.'

They were both graduates and had been employed in Hut 6 because of their supposed intelligence and discretion but they had broken that trust and she had no choice but to tell them they were being dismissed immediately. Mary tried to plead with her but she was wasting her time and within minutes they'd both left Hut 6 and were on their way out of Bletchley Park, never to return. Mair felt ill and frightened by the sudden way in which the axe had fallen on two friends and colleagues.

'I had never seen anything like this before. There was absolutely no mercy shown, no second chance offered. They had broken the rules and they must pay for it. I tentatively looked around the room and everybody else looked bewildered and anxious. I think we were all close to tears.'

Sink the *Bismarck*

Sally Norton's first contact with Nazi Germany came in 1937 when her parents sent her to Munich to improve her German. She'd been brought up at her mother's Scottish ancestral home, Gilmerton House, a beautiful eighteenth-century mansion around twenty miles east of Edinburgh. It was a very comfortable childhood. Her grandfather was the 5th Lord Grantley and, like many young girls from upper-class families, Sally – whose formal name was the more refined Sarah – didn't go to school. She was taught German, French and Italian by a succession of governesses and hated them all. 'But I think they gave me a pretty good education, especially in languages.'

Despite her ability to speak German, Munich was the very last place Sally wanted to go. She was seventeen, had a mind of her own, and didn't share the obsession with Hitler of some young, upper-class women – Unity and Diana Mitford being perhaps the best-known examples. She couldn't see how going to Nazi Germany could improve anyone.

'I went reluctantly and with bad grace because I really wanted to go to Italy. My innocent mind was full of fantasies of romantic Italian boys, but my mother dismissed them as unsuitable for my tender age and I was dispatched to Germany forthwith.'

She was sent to stay with a Bavarian *Graf* and *Gräfin*, a duke and duchess, who were kind and welcoming to her, although they pretended they couldn't speak English in order to force Sally and the two other British girls who were staying with them to speak German. 'They were very anti-Nazi, although of course they didn't admit it openly, and they were lovely. I hated everything else about Germany. The streets were full of people in uniforms strutting around in jackboots.'

As their understanding of the language improved, the girls became very angry over the behaviour of the Nazis. It was to lead to a minor diplomatic incident that would see Sally sent home in disgrace. She and her friends were particularly incensed with the 'odious' anti-Jewish newspaper *Der Stürmer*, which even top Nazis like Herman Göring criticised – it was not allowed in any of the departments he controlled. *Der Stürmer* was read by a small minority of largely ill-educated people, but because it had Hitler's support it was pinned up in glass-covered display cases in every city for everyone to read. Munich, the spiritual home of the Nazi movement, was no exception. Sally and her friends were shocked by its virulent attacks on the Jews.

'It was both vicious and destructive. Myself and other like-minded English girls also studying the language were outraged by this obscenity and the seventeen-year-old energy was detonated by the unjust and atrocious persecution of the Jewish people.'

They began a crusade against the Nazis, initially walking around the main Odeonsplatz square ignoring Nazi salutes, but given that they were young girls, and foreigners to boot, there was little anyone felt inclined to do about that. Since no one seemed to care about their refusal to make Nazi salutes, they soon gave up on that tack and launched a campaign against the *Der Stürmer* display cases.

'The plan, hardly a plot, was to secure a hammer, sneak out at night, smash the glass and tear down the offensive publication from its frame. The stage was set nearby in Durchstrasse. The scene, a street corner. We struck the glass in the display case in the middle of the frame, pulled down and tore up the filthy newspaper and went on to the next target. That was when the fun began.'

The noise of shattering glass that had nothing to do with their own attacks on Jewish shops and businesses alerted a gang of baton-wielding Stormtroopers who chased the girls around the streets, but their jackboots were a hindrance and the young girls, all wearing gym shoes, ran off in different directions, evading them easily.

'After a few nights of this hedonistic action, the glass was suddenly replaced by wire mesh, which was a slight hindrance but overcome by purchasing a pair of wire cutters from an ironmonger in another district; this process of removal took longer and scouts had to be posted at intervals.'

But the Stormtroopers, no doubt imagining that they faced a dangerous student opposition group, were not prepared to be outwitted by young girls.

'In the end, of course, we were caught, giving grounds for embarrassment to our Foreign Office, who were trying to be congenial to the Germans, and were sent home in disrepute.'

Although she was now fluent in German, the Second World War was still a couple of years away and she had to negotiate the 'season', a prospect which did not fill Sally with quite the same degree of dread that it had Jane Hughes. It was, after all, something that she'd always expected to do, even looked forward to. Her grandfather was a peer of the realm, whom her father would succeed in 1943. Her godfather was Lord Louis Mountbatten and her mother's family, the Kinlochs, were the local lairds in East Lothian. Queen Mary, the King's mother, was a friend of her grandmother and frequently came to tea at her grandmother's elegant house in Eaton Place.

'When I was about four years old, I was summoned to the drawing room from our nursery on the fourth floor to meet Queen Mary. Clutching on to Nanny, who had to wait outside the door, I was gently pushed into her presence. As I advanced towards this formidable lady my knickers fell down. Apparently, I calmly stepped out of them as if nothing had happened. Queen Mary laughed with pleasure and poor Nanny was mortified.'

To ensure there were no such embarrassments when Sally was presented to Queen Mary's daughter-in-law Queen Elizabeth, she was dispatched to Miss Vacani's, an expensive and very classy dance school for young women. Miss Vacani had schooled the young Princesses Elizabeth and Margaret in the art of deportment; now Sally was to be taught how to curtsey.

'I thought this curtseying business was going to be a doddle. This supposedly easy obeisance to the King and Queen was actually profoundly difficult. You had to bring your left leg behind your right leg, bend the knee almost down to the floor, keeping your head high and eyes straight forward. Going down was not too bad, but coming up was almost impossible without wobbling. Such an error Miss Vacani would not countenance. It took hours of practice to become perfect and I'm not sure I ever got it right, but at least I got rid of the wobble.'

She was forced to wear a very traditional and very expensive ivory satin dress with a train and puff sleeves. 'I hated it, but no amount of sulking and remonstrations that it was unfashionable would change my mother's mind.' The day of presentation came, with a Rolls-Royce delivering Sally and her parents at the Sovereign's entrance of Buckingham Palace. The twenty or so young debutantes were shown into an ante-room and told by a gentleman usher that he would call them in one by one.

'I started to shake and feel sick but there was no going back now, no escape. I heard my name called. Chin up, shoulders down, I began to walk forward. I had a blurred vision of a mass of people to my right; presumably my parents were among them. Twelve paces forward and there on the left were the Queen and the King.'

Sally curtseyed to the Queen first, without a wobble, but when she saw the familiar face of Queen Mary standing behind the royal couple she curtseyed to her grandmother's friend before curtseying to King George, a breach of etiquette that brought a subsequent reprimand from the head usher.

'The rest of my debutante year remains largely out of focus and seemed to blend into one long dance. On arrival at a dance you were given a small rectangular card which folded, with a small pencil attached by a silken cord. The card was numbered from one to twenty and the men had to ask you if you would dance with them. It seems amazing to me now that we managed to keep going night after night, and it wasn't just the dances. There were lunches as well, almost every day. We weren't allowed to dress in a sloppy way. You always wore white gloves to go out to lunch – always.'

She wore a different dress to each event and they were much more fashionable ones, made for her by Victor Stiebel, one of Britain's most famous designers, who was so fascinated by the possibilities of Sally's long legs and 18½-inch waist that he dressed her for free, while her godfather Lord Louis Mountbatten paid for a 'wonderful' Coming Out Ball at his Park Lane home.

The onset of war saw Sally working as a journalist for *Vogue* magazine, for five shillings a week (which barely covered the cost of travel), while writing dispatches from London for the *Baltimore Sun*. But eventually she and her close friend and fellow debutante Osla Benning, then regarded as one of the most beautiful women in London, decided to go to Slough and work at the Hawker Siddeley aircraft factory, which was building Hurricane fighter aircraft for the RAF.

'Osla and I wanted to do something really important, and we thought: making aeroplanes. So we trooped off to the Slough trading estate – ghastly place – and said here we are. We want to make an aeroplane.'

They lived with Sally's father, Richard, now separated from her mother and working as an executive at Pinewood Studios. He had a cottage nearby and it was here that Sally introduced Osla to a young man who was to be her boyfriend for the next three years. Lord Mountbatten had asked his goddaughter if she could find a girlfriend for his young nephew, Prince Philip of Greece.

'Uncle Dickie said to me: "I don't think Philip's got a girlfriend at the moment. I wish you could find a nice girl for him because he doesn't know anyone." Osla didn't have a boyfriend at the time, so I said: "I know, I'll get them together."'

Early in 1941, Sally and Osla, who was also fluent in German, received a letter ordering them to report to Bletchley Park, to Commander Denniston's deputy Edward Travis. Having spent most of her life in a magnificent country house designed by William Adam, Sally was distinctly unimpressed by the Bletchley mansion – 'an ugly Victorian monstrosity' – where Commander Travis welcomed them and told them they would be working in the German Naval Section in Hut 4.

Probably because of their backgrounds, they were put up in a beautiful Queen Anne house in Aspley Guise eight miles to the east of Bletchley Park. 'We were very lucky, Osla and I. We were billeted with two darling elderly people who looked after us beautifully. They were marvellous really, very good to us. Kind. They never complained. The large garden was unattended except for vegetables and in the summer the grass grew so long you could sunbathe topless without being seen.'

Sally and Osla's initial role was alongside a number of other well-to-do women working in the Index, logging down various details from the decoded messages, such as facts about individual U-boats, on file cards held in what looked like long shoe boxes.

'Each time a signal came in and was translated, you had to put down the salient points in that signal, such as the name of the U-boat commander on one card, the number of the U-boat on another, the coordinates or the person; anything related to that signal went on different cards. Nobody explained anything. Within a couple of days we realised that this information had been obtained by codebreaking but even then we had no idea of the whole picture.'

The Index had to be operational twenty-four hours a day, so they worked in two shifts, a day shift and a very long night shift. 'The night watches were pretty awful. They were called watches because we were the Naval Section and the navy has watches not shifts.'

On their days off, they rushed up to London on the train, making the most of every minute. Sally was going out with Billy Cavendish, the Marquess of Hartington, one of the most eligible bachelors in the country, who had taken a commission in the Coldstream Guards.

'Sometimes boyfriends would be back from the war and you always managed to keep in touch. The most lovely man, Mr Gibbs, the head hall porter at Claridge's, knew exactly where all our boyfriends were. He used to say: "Hello, Miss Norton. Lord Hartington's back. He said he would see you here later. I think he said six o'clock." So of course I was back there by six o'clock. It was so nice to have a boyfriend.'

But there was absolutely no way that any of them were prepared to have sex before marriage.

'We just didn't think of that at all. We were brought up to what my mother used to call "behave nicely". The boys could kiss you on the cheek, but not much more. We knew what the more daring girls were doing but as far as I was concerned it was all much too frightening for me to do it. You were supposed to go to the marriage bed as a virgin. There was no such thing as birth control so if a girl got pregnant, she married almost immediately.'

Their favourite haunt was the 400, a nightclub on Leicester Square where you could dance all night. It was very small, but it was members only and there was live music every night.

'As days off were so precious and time so short I usually took the milk train from Euston back to Bletchley at five o'clock in the morning, arriving in time for the 9am watch a bit bleary-eyed and hoping the head of the watch would find my work satisfactory and not notice I was a bit overdressed.'

The intelligence on the German U-Boats and the attacks on the Allied convoys was still coming mainly from the messages that Jocelyn Bostock was working on.

'We did in fact derive some valuable information about German naval operations. The first time we actually saw the [original] contents of an Enigma naval signal, as I vividly remember, was when the logbook of a patrol boat captured in the North Sea became available to us.'

She and Susie Henderson had been joined by a young man called Harry Hinsley, one of the students recruited from Cambridge. Slight and bespectacled, he came from Walsall in the Black Country, where his father drove a horse and cart for the local ironworks. Phoebe Senyard immediately developed a soft spot for him.

'I can remember quite well showing Harry some of the sorting and how delighted he seemed when he began to recognise the different types of signals. Those were very enjoyable days indeed. We were all very happy and cheerful, working in close cooperation with each other. If I was in difficulty, I knew I could go to Harry.'

The intelligence analysts in the Admiralty, who plotted the movements of enemy shipping, were ignoring Jocelyn and Susie and the increasing amount of intelligence they were managing to glean from the German naval messages intercepted by the wireless sites at Winchester and Scarborough. The Admiralty intelligence experts didn't understand how Hut 4 had worked out the intelligence, so they didn't believe it. Jocelyn hoped that if they wouldn't listen to her or Susie, they might at least listen to Harry, given that he was a man. But it made no difference. Two young girls and a student in corduroys, what would they know?

'Harry had the greatest difficulty in convincing the Naval Intelligence Department in the Admiralty that this intelligence was sound,' Jocelyn recalled. 'They regarded Bletchley as a peculiar set-up, made up of eccentric boffins, some of whom were very young, and most of whom were mere civilians, and undisciplined at that.'

The situation came to a head in June 1940. Harry, Jocelyn and Susie had been reporting that the German battlecruisers *Gneisenau* and *Scharnhorst* had left the Baltic to track the Royal Navy's Home Fleet. The Admiralty refused to tell the Home Fleet because their analysts didn't agree. On Friday 7 June 1940, Harry spent much of the day trying to persuade the duty captain to send out a warning. He refused. On the following day, the *Gneisenau* and the *Scharnhorst* attacked the Royal Navy's aircraft carrier HMS *Glorious* and her escorts, the destroyers HMS *Acasta* and HMS *Ardent*. All three British ships were sunk in just over two hours, with the loss of more than 1,500 officers and men.

By the time Sally and Osla arrived in Hut 4 in early 1941, the relationship with the Admiralty had begun to improve, but it didn't take long for the rows to start all over again. They resurfaced in May 1941, when the Royal Navy was tracking the new German battleship the *Bismarck*, the pride of the German Navy. On the morning of Saturday 24 May 1941, the British battleship *Prince of Wales* and the battlecruiser *Hood* took on the *Bismarck* and the German heavy cruiser *Prinz Eugen* in the Battle of the Denmark Strait between Iceland and Greenland. The *Hood* was hit and sunk, while the *Prince of Wales* was forced to withdraw.

Despite the German victory, the *Bismarck* was badly damaged and it was soon clear to Harry, Jocelyn and Susie from the *Bismarck*'s radio messages that it was being controlled from Paris rather than the German Navy's headquarters in Wilhelmshaven. They'd seen this before and they knew it only happened when a German ship was heading for a French port, in this case almost certainly Brest where it could be repaired. But this had been missed by the Admiralty's intelligence analysts.

Harry rang them, winding the handle on the old-fashioned telephone that provided a direct line between Hut 4 and the Admiralty. He eventually got hold of someone who didn't really want to speak to him. Didn't he know they were busy? They were trying to find the *Bismarck*. It was somewhere in the Atlantic, probably making for Norway. No, Harry said. It was definitely heading for France.

Yet again, as with the *Glorious*, the Bletchley Park assessment contradicted the Admiralty's assumptions, so they refused to pass it on to the Royal Navy commanders. It was not until the early evening of Sunday 25 May, following yet another heated telephone conversation between Harry and the Admiralty's analysts, that they finally accepted that Bletchley was right and told the fleet they should assume the *Bismarck* was heading for Brest.

Meanwhile, Jane Hughes had just come on shift in the Hut 6 Decoding Room where she and her colleagues were briefed on the latest situation concerning the *Bismarck*.

'We all knew that we'd got the fleet out in the Atlantic trying to locate her because she was the Germans' most important, latest battleship and had better guns and so on than anybody else, and she'd already sunk the *Hood*. So it was vitally important to find where she was and try to get rid of her.'

Just over an hour into her shift, Jane was typing out a message on the main Luftwaffe Enigma, the Red. She'd set up her Typex machine to decode the message and a stream of German was coming out. She was typing automatically so she wasn't actually reading the German. Then suddenly she spotted the word Brest.

'I thought, Brest, that's interesting. I wonder what that's about.'

Jane read the message in full and realised that it was from the Luftwaffe headquarters in Berlin telling someone important that the *Bismarck* was heading for the French port of Brest.

She immediately called in one of the codebreakers, Keith Batey, and explained what it said. A Luftwaffe general whose son was on the *Bismarck* had asked if he was all right and had been told that the German battleship was heading for France. It was rushed through to the intelligence reporters who immediately sent out an urgent top-secret message: 'Information received graded A1 that intention of *Bismarck* is to head for the west coast of France.'

A1 was the highest grade they could give the intelligence. It meant that there was absolutely no doubt. In a moment of pure drama, the message from Bletchley arrived in the Admiralty just seven minutes after the analysts there finally accepted Harry's insistence that the *Bismarck* was heading for Brest. The next day, a Catalina flying boat sent up as a direct result of the intelligence provided by Bletchley spotted the *Bismarck*. The Royal Navy chased her down and eventually she was sunk. It was an important victory which owed a great deal to Bletchley, and because the work being carried out by Harry, Jocelyn and Susie was not top secret like the work being done in Hut 6, the other codebreakers could be told about that part of it. It was the first time they had seen tangible evidence that their work was having an impact on the war. There was a rousing cheer in the dining room in the mansion when the BBC reported that the *Bismarck* had been sunk.

Mavis Lever, who was also working at Bletchley, was Keith Batey's girlfriend at the time and later his wife. When the film *Sink the Bismarck* was released in 1960, she took their young son to see it. She saw the ship begin to sink on the screen and had to look away.

'I really did feel quite sick. I was thinking how awful it was that one's breaking of a message could send so many people to the bottom. But that was war and that was the way we had to play it. If we thought about it too much we should never have been able to cope.'

By the summer of 1942, Hut 4 was crammed full of people and new concrete and brick blocks were being built to rehouse the codebreaking sections. Phoebe couldn't wait to move. 'We were very crowded now and had spread to Hut 5 and parts of the house nearest Hut 4. So we were all longing for the day when we should be moving to our new brick-built home by the lake. They were very happy days although we were so huddled together, working so hard and under such difficulties owing to the lack of space, but we seemed to jog along in harmony, everyone being friendly and cooperative.'

The Naval Section moved into Block A and Block B on the other side of the lake in late 1942. For security reasons they continued to call themselves Hut 4, rather than Naval

Section, to disguise the fact that Bletchley was breaking the German Navy's top codes.

Sally only got into really serious trouble on one occasion. She was working in the Index Room one morning when she heard footsteps outside and in walked her godfather Lord Louis Mountbatten, now Chief of Combined Operations, followed by a group of harassed-looking Bletchley managers.

'I managed to splutter in my astonishment, "Uncle Dickie, what are you doing here?"'

'Oh, I knew you were here and I thought I'd see how you were getting on. Show me the system of your cross-reference index.'

Sally's cheeks were bright red with embarrassment as she explained how the Index worked to her godfather, only too aware of the anger of the senior managers behind her at this young woman's impertinence in disrupting their carefully planned programme.

'I was awfully pleased to see Uncle Dickie and, as the Index was considered fairly lowly work, all of us on watch were thrilled.'

But first thing next morning she was ordered to report to Commander Travis, who tore her off a strip for daring to ask the Chief of Combined Operations to visit the Index.

'I assured him, eyes full of tears, that I knew nothing of the visit and he was my godfather. Bless him, he lent me a hankie to blow my nose.'

In August 1943, Sally's grandfather died and her father became the 6th Lord Grantley, Baron of Markenfield, making her the Honourable Miss Sarah Norton.

'It got out that I was an honourable and I was frightfully embarrassed by this. Somebody came up to me: "I hear that you're an honourable." I was fed up to the back teeth with it. I said, "No I'm not. I'm very dishonourable, so shut up."'

The actress Pamela Gibson, also a German linguist, worked alongside Sally and Osla in the Hut 4 Index.

'I had a letter from a rather interfering godmother who said she was sure I was doing splendid work entertaining the troops but she knew a girl who had just gone to a very secret place and was doing fascinating work and they needed people with languages. That made me feel I was fiddling while Rome burned. So I wrote off to the address they sent me and thought no more about it. I had just been offered a part in a play when I got a telegram from Frank Birch asking me to meet him at the Admiralty. He gave me several tests and said, "Well, I suppose we could offer you a job," and I said, "Well, you know about the stage, what would you do if you were me?" He said: "The stage can wait, the war can't." So I went to Bletchley.'

The Index had started off with a few shoe boxes and by the end of the war, by which time Pamela was in charge of it all, had expanded to fill three large rooms. But initially, she found the work depressing. She'd expected the offer of a role in naval intelligence to be more interesting than cross-referencing the numbers of the U-boats and the names of German naval officers.

'I slightly resented it, giving up the stage where I was enjoying myself and doing what I really wanted to do, because I thought that I was going to be doing something a bit more exciting than indexing. I thought I was going to be dropped in France or something.'

Like many people at Bletchley, she sought an escape from the frustrations of her work in the social life of the Park and in particular the musical and dramatic clubs, where her professional expertise made her one of the stars, albeit among a number of other prominent people, including other actors and several leading musicians and writers.

'We gave what we thought were splendid parties. A girl called Maxine Birley, the Comtesse de la Falaise as she became, was a great beauty and mad about France and I remember her giving a party at which we all had to be very French. People would change partners quite a lot. We were rather contained in a way-out place and you could only travel if you managed to get transport so there was a good deal of changing of partners.'

The drama and musical clubs combined at Christmas to put on a revue, which was always very popular because of the standard of the writing, the music and the performances. It was while working on the revue for Christmas 1943 that Pamela met and fell in love with her future husband, Jim Rose; he was one of the intelligence reporters and wrote a sketch in which she took the female lead. Jim was due to be away on duty when the revue took place so he was allowed to watch the rehearsal.

'No one was allowed to go to rehearsals but at that time I was going to Washington just before Christmas so I was allowed in and this glorious vision of loveliness stepped down from the stage and said: "Your sketch isn't bad."'

Phoebe, now in charge of the distribution of all the various messages that were coming into Hut 4 – very far from the basic secretary she had been when she first started work at Broadway Buildings before the war – encouraged the junior staff in her section to put up Christmas decorations.

'Mr Birch gave a wonderful luncheon party to the heads of sub-sections and all the old staff. Mr Birch, Susie and I, being the veterans of the sections, had a special little ceremony all to ourselves in a corner of the room where we toasted the Naval Section and anything else which came into our heads. It was great fun and it was our own special celebration. By the time we went into the room where the luncheon was served, we were almost prepared for anything, but not for the wonderful sight that met our eyes. The tables were positively groaning with Christmas fare. They were arranged in a T-shape, the table which formed the top of the T was loaded with turkey, geese and chicken whilst the table down the centre at which we all sat was decorated with game pie, and fruit salad, cheese and various other dishes. Each person had a menu, which was afterwards signed by everyone there, and we set to and thoroughly enjoyed ourselves, and I know that I was still beaming at the end of the day and feeling exceedingly happy.'

Meanwhile, Prince Philip was spending the Christmas period at Windsor Castle, where the seventeen-year-old Princess Elizabeth and he enjoyed a mutual attraction. Shortly afterwards, he and Osla split up. On the rebound, she became engaged to a diplomat, but it didn't last. Unsurprisingly for two young women in their early twenties, with many young male friends all going off to war, and the intensity of their relationships heightened by the possibility that they might never come back, the love lives of both Osla and Sally enjoyed numerous ups and downs with what Sally described as 'magnified highs and lows, either enraptured or suicidal'. Osla had come back from leave with a large emerald engagement ring given to her by the diplomat.

'Two months later, the despicable cad changed his mind,' said Sally. 'Osla tearfully returned the ring swearing she had never liked green stones anyway. I got engaged to a handsome officer in the Coldstream Guards, but was soon disengaged by both families who thought we were too young and anyway it was wartime. What that had to do with it escaped me, but my heart was broken for the first time.'

The handsome Coldstream Guards officer was her long-time boyfriend Billy Cavendish. After the break-up enforced by their parents, he fell in love with Kathleen Kennedy, the sister of John F. Kennedy, the future US President, and married her. Sally's heart was broken a second time.

'I felt it would never survive the anguish and when he was killed in France the misery was compounded.'

But there were lighter moments. One afternoon, when their watch was over and they were waiting for transport to take them back to their billets, Osla and Sally decided to send their friend Jean Campbell-Harris down one of the long corridors, which ran downhill, in one of the laundry baskets the decoded messages were delivered in.

'We launched it down the corridor where it gathered momentum by the second. To our horror, at the T-junction,

Jean suddenly disappeared, basket and all, through some double swing doors.'

Sally would dine out on the claim that the basket carrying a giggling Jean had careered into the gents' loo, but in fact it burst into the office of Commander Geoffrey Tandy, the head of technical intelligence, who had already shown his irritation at the girls' willingness to enjoy themselves when there was a lull in the work. Jean took the brunt of his anger.

'Geoffrey Tandy had already decided he did not like me and now he was absolutely furious. As a punishment the three of us were taken off the same shift and it took us three weeks to get back together again.'

Jean had arrived a few months after Sally and Osla, but although the need for more people was becoming urgent, recruitment was still largely targeting people who were known to come from reliable families.

'They were really frightfully snobbish about the girls who worked there. A friend of my father's said: "Maybe when Jean's finished her secretarial course she would like to go to a place called Bletchley."

'Sally and I were great pals but I think Osla was my dearest friend. She was a delight. Spoiled rotten, but adorable and loved by everyone. She had dark hair and fair skin and was simply beautiful. Her mother had no home but lived in a permanent flat in Claridge's and had had five husbands.'

Geoffrey Tandy, who was in his early forties, was in charge of captured enemy documents. He was a former curator

at the Natural History Museum and had access to special
materials used in the preservation of old documents. An
officer on the Royal Naval Reserve, he had been sent to
Bletchley Park because he was an expert in cryptograms,
not – as the Admiralty clearly assumed – encoded messages,
but mosses, ferns, algae, lichens and fungi.

Peggy Senior, who worked alongside Mr Tandy translating the documents, was recruited aged twenty-one as a
Foreign Office linguist, having studied German at Girton
College, Cambridge. The Admiralty might have made a
mistake in its interpretation of Tandy's skills but so far as
Peggy was concerned it was a good decision to send him
to Bletchley.

'They couldn't have done a better thing for him
because he found it a romantic thing altogether. It really
thrilled him generally. It was like a small boy. My friend
and I were typing up the message that was sent to all the
German fleet and he said: "If you don't feel romance now,
God help you." So, strange as he was, he was a romantic
at heart.'

Tandy's Technical Intelligence Section also kept track
of the latest detail of all the various U-boats and Peggy was
in charge of a log-book which included any information
they could find in the intercepted messages about every
submarine. It created an odd connection between the
women extracting the detail from the messages and the
individual U-boats, almost like sports fans following a
specific team.

'The thing I look back on with pleasure is my U-boat
log. You wrote on each U-boat's page its number and its

type, name of its commander, what torpedoes it had fired. Did they hit the target? Did they sink it? And what stocks had they got left? So I got to know quite a bit about the submarine war. You got quite interested in individual U-boats for no reason at all. A particular number took your fancy and you wanted to know how it got on. We all had our favourite U-boats.'

Commander Travis's daughter Valerie was in charge of the library containing all the captured documents, known as 'pinches' because they'd been 'stolen' from the enemy. Some were codebooks and operator instructions that would help to break other codes while others were technical documents that provided the correct terms for new or obscure pieces of equipment that would help the people translating the messages.

'It was the only way of finding the German terms for all their extraordinary torpedoes and things and finding out a bit about them, so as I had Italian and German, I was given the job of collating all these documents and listing them. We had P numbers for the pinches: PG numbers for the German and PI for the Italian, and of course eventually we had a Japanese as well.'

With people who spoke good German at a premium, Sally was promoted to the German Operational Watch, translating the lower-level naval messages. Her new boss was a Royal Navy commander who was a good deal older than the women working for him.

'He was very nice and he tried to keep us under control. Wasn't always easy for him, but he did. At that age you do get very mischievous, I'm afraid. That kept morale high and the work did too because you knew what you were translating was terribly important. I make it sound as if we were silly little girls but actually we weren't and we did work incredibly hard.

'You were translating German decrypts and you'd really got to know how to do them pretty quickly if you had the lingo. So we were reading lots about U-boats and that sort of thing, Atlantic convoys in such danger. It was a nightmare. An absolute nightmare. It brought an edge of urgency to the work. I remember thinking, I'm not going to go one by one by one until I get to the bottom. I'm going to find the ones about the U-boats first. Because the U-boats were always signalling to each other where they were so it was very important the Admiralty got that.'

Sheila Mackenzie was in her second year at Aberdeen University in 1943 reading modern languages. She was already on a reserved list to teach French and German, which prevented her being called up for the armed forces, but she didn't want to be stuck teaching when all her friends were off 'doing something about Hitler'. So she took her name off the teaching list, and within a couple of weeks received a letter from the Foreign Office inviting her to an interview in London.

'At the age of nineteen coming up to twenty, I'd never been out of Scotland. Money was scarce, travelling was not encouraged. Things were very, very difficult. So I rejoiced to go down to London and I had my interview and I saw as much of central London as I could in the time allowed and shortly after that I got another letter asking me to report to Bletchley, and when I got there I was to telephone, and the voice at the other end said: "Ah, yes, Miss Mackenzie, we're expecting you." And that was it.'

She was sent to work in Hut 4 on low-level German codes, which were relatively easy to break and involved messages for heavy German guns and radar stations along the French, Belgian, Dutch and Mediterranean coasts. 'I remember thinking, this is interesting. They got a lot of messages in. I just collected them from the teleprinter room once or twice daily and worked my way through them. I decoded them and translated them. It was weather reports, sightings of ships, sightings of aircraft, just warning the radar stations and gun emplacements what was happening. I would have liked to have known more but you couldn't. It was impressed on me that security was absolutely essential. I didn't ask too many questions. It was not the done thing.'

In her spare time, Sheila joined the Scottish Reels Club and it was there she met the love of her life. Oliver Lawn was one of the Hut 6 codebreakers and often stood in for Hugh Foss when he was away. 'I first saw Oliver at the Reels Club. I used to love reels and I noticed that when Hugh Foss was absent, Oliver took the class. And I remember this rather nice lad. He was tall, elegant and danced beautifully. I suppose we danced together and Oliver thought that I was an adequate partner for him.

'We went down to Stratford on one occasion and we went to a play and then we went for a picnic on the river. I remember I couldn't buy much but I bought lettuce and things to eat and I think my billeter had given me something and we had a picnic on the river and of course the clouds came over and we had a terrific thunderstorm come down and I was absolutely soaked. He asked me if I was all right. I said: "No I am not."'

As the need for staff grew, it was no longer possible to get enough women from the upper classes who spoke German to fill the various roles. But the introduction of conscription for women gave the Admiralty large numbers of additional members of the Women's Royal Naval Service, the Wrens, and when they began arriving at Bletchley in 1941, it was only natural that some of them would be sent to work in the Naval Section.

Jean Tocher had spent a year at Darmstadt studying German before the war. When she joined the Wrens she was sent to Bletchley to work on the Naval Section's 'Allied Plot', which was a chart of the world covering all four walls of one room on which a number of Wrens plotted the movement of all the Allied ships and their German, Italian and Japanese counterparts.

'These huge charts were being used to plot where the German ships were and where the U-boats were going to attack our ships, so that the RAF could be sent out or evasive action taken – it was the sharp end of the naval war that we were, in our very small way, involved in.'

Initially, the women working on the Plot reported any potential threats direct to the RAF by scrambler phone. But the Admiralty didn't like Hut 4 talking directly to the RAF about naval issues, so by the time Jean arrived the threats were being reported by phone to MI6, which passed them on to the RAF as intelligence reports. Jean was twenty-five and a bit older and more confident than the other Wrens so she was appointed as the head of one of the watches.

'We got secret and top-secret messages and every day we were hastily plotting all the convoys. We had a colour code: blue for cruisers, green for destroyers, purple for frigates and pink for corvettes, and there were other pins which had a piece of white cardboard in the middle and on that we would put the number of the convoy. It had to be absolutely accurate and quick so that, when a German code had been cracked, you could see U-boats moving towards a convoy.'

Like many of the Wrens working at Bletchley Park, Jean was based at Woburn Abbey, the country seat of the Duke of Bedford, which had been taken over by the government for the duration of the war, and bussed into Bletchley for each watch. They used naval terms for everything they did, so the shifts were watches, their dormitories were cabins, their living quarters were the fo'c'sle, and the area in front of the Abbey was the quarterdeck.

'We were billeted in the servants' quarters, eight double bunks to a room, the bats flew in and the condensation dripped off the ceilings. There were about four bathrooms and you couldn't have a bath in privacy, because there weren't enough places to wash – there were enamel basins on a shelf, so you had to leave the door open so other Wrens could use the basins to do their washing while you were having a bath, it was all a bit like boarding school.'

In late 1944, Sally was selected for a new top-secret job. The difficulties dealing with the Admiralty simply wouldn't go away. Frank Birch called Sally into his office and told her she was to be part of a team charged with improving relations with the Admiralty. It would be based right inside the Admiralty's Operational Intelligence Centre and would be staffed by four young women, with one of them on duty at all times, and part of their job would be to 'smile prettily' at the admirals in order to get them onside.

'I managed to blurt out: "Sir, are you giving me this job for my brains or my exceptionally good legs?" To which he replied, "A bit of both will come in handy."'

Sally would be based in London, just a taxi ride away from the clubs and hotels where all her friends met, and could live in the flat of a great-uncle who had moved out for the war. It was 'a dream come true' – a flat just off Piccadilly, just around the corner from the Ritz, and looking out over St James's Park.

'The Admiralty was about the best job any girl could have. The responsibility was awesome – you were alone in this room, completely responsible for every decrypt that came from Bletchley and you had to decide who saw it. No one was allowed into our room, not even an admiral. All the telephones were scramblers and I had a direct line to the Prime Minister. Four girls and one nice man called Bill, who was really our boss, working round the clock, and all those lovely sailors in the passages.'

4

The Wrens Arrive

Morag Maclennan was one of the first Wrens to arrive at Bletchley Park in early 1941 as the number of recruits needed forced the authorities to spread their net far wider. They were no longer simply taking academics and young women from 'good families' who could be trusted to keep the secret. They were looking for young women from any background so long as they had the necessary intelligence and ability to 'keep Mum'.

Eight Wrens were brought in as a trial measure to work in Hut 11 operating the Bombes, the top-secret machines that tested various Enigma settings potentially being used by the Germans. These machines were vital if Hut 6 and the naval codebreakers in Hut 8 were to be able to break the codes quickly enough to get the intelligence to British military and naval commanders in time.

Morag and her friends had joined the Wrens because they wanted to do their bit and liked the idea of being near the sea. There was, of course, the added attraction of meeting young sailors. For Morag herself, the navy was in her blood. Her brother was a marine engineer and already in the navy, as were a number of her cousins.

'We used to go up to the Clyde a lot and go round on Clyde steamers so I was very enthusiastic about ships and the sea. There was a long lag between when I applied, several months I was waiting, looking forward to it and reading snippets about things that were happening and thinking, gosh, this is going to be interesting, being in a port and big ships and all that kind of excitement – that's what I was looking forward to.'

The Women's Royal Naval Service was initially set up during the First World War and disbanded when the war came to an end. But as the prospects of another war with Germany increased in 1938, the Wrens were re-formed, with advertisements for volunteers drawing in large numbers of women, including some who had served during the First World War and had persuaded their daughters to join as well. Like the other women's services, the WAAF and the ATS, the Wrens really took off after conscription for women was introduced in 1941.

There were three separate sites where all Wrens received their basic training: Mill Hill in north London, Wesley College at Headingley in Leeds, and Tullichewan Castle by Loch Lomond in Scotland. There were only three weeks to train each 'draft' so the instructors concentrated on testing the girls' ability to obey orders and making them feel that even though they weren't allowed to go to sea they were still part of the Royal Navy. Everything had a naval term, based on the concept of being on a ship. The Wrens slept in 'cabins' on 'bunks' not beds. The floor was the 'deck'. The kitchen was the 'galley', the dining room the 'mess', or for officers the 'wardroom'. Time off was 'shore leave'.

Morag was told to report to the railway station and only then to open her travel warrant to find out where she was going.

'I was hoping it would be Portsmouth or Plymouth or somewhere, so to find that it said Bletchley was a terrible disappointment. We got off at the station and somebody met us. We went up a little gravel path straight into Hut 11 and there were all these machines there and we were told what we were going to do, and it was quite obvious that there was no escape.'

The Bombes were built by the British Tabulating Machine Company (BTM). There were only four Bombes in Hut 11 when Morag arrived and up until that point they had been operated by BTM staff co-opted into the RAF. But the codebreakers knew they would need many more and had ordered an initial batch of seventy. They would need around 700 people to run them and BTM didn't have that many men to spare. They needed them to build the machines, which is why Bletchley Park had been forced to call in the Wrens.

Initially, Morag and the other Wrens were allowed to wear civilian clothes to blend in with the rest of the staff at Bletchley, most of whom were civilians, a lot of them young academics or former students who wore very casual clothes. So all the members of the armed forces who worked at Bletchley wore civilian clothes, whatever rank they were. Rank meant very little among the codebreakers in any case. Everyone was treated on the basis of the job regardless of whether they were an officer, a sergeant or just a basic airman, sailor or soldier. Then an admiral came to visit Bletchley and wanted to know where all his Wrens were. When a number of young women in civilian clothes were pointed out to him, he blew his top. 'It's disgraceful,' he said. 'My Wrens should be jumping up, hands down seams of skirts.' He went back to London on a mission, determined to sort out the lax discipline at Bletchley, and from then on everyone in the armed forces was forced to wear uniform to work.

The Bombes were proving their worth and more and more were needed, along with more and more Wrens to operate them. Dozens of Bombes were installed in country houses around Bletchley Park which were specially requisitioned as bases for the machines themselves and as accommodation for the hundreds of Wrens who would be operating them. Some of these country mansions were very beautiful, others were close to derelict. The first five, at Steeple Claydon, Walton Hall, Crawley Grange, Wavendon House and Gayhurst Manor, were all taken over by Bletchley in 1942.

Soon the authorities were forced to look further afield, creating a custom-built site capable of housing more than 60 Bombes and 600 Wrens at Stanmore, north of London. The need for more staff to run the Bombes was acute and the authorities began to advertise for Wrens 'for interesting and extremely important work . . . necessitating the operating of light electrical machinery. Girls should be of good physique and education, quick, accurate and keen, with good powers of concentration.'

Colette St George-Yorke became a Wren in October 1943 when just seventeen and a half, the earliest age at which you could join up. Colette had been brought up in Harrogate in Yorkshire and went to the local convent school. Her father was a timber merchant, but because of the war the government had taken over all the buying and selling of timber and he was working for the Ministry of Aircraft Production. When Colette left school she was mad keen on becoming a Wren but she was only sixteen and had to do something else until she was old enough to join up.

'The chap who lived next door to us in Harrogate was the managing director of the Yorkshire Dyeware and Chemical Company in Leeds and he said there was a job for me. I could be a lab assistant. So I was there for a year until I was seventeen and a half and could officially apply to join the Wrens.'

Colette signed up and was given a medical and sent home. A couple of weeks later she was called forward to the training and drafting depot at Mill Hill.

'And I thought it was absolutely marvellous. They had a quarterdeck and a white ensign. You couldn't walk across the quarterdeck. You had to go at the double. If you went across the quarterdeck you had to salute the white ensign.'

The Wrens were organised into different divisions, each given the name of a famous naval hero. Colette was in Howe Division, named after the eighteenth-century Admiral of the Fleet Richard Howe who defeated the French at the Battle of the Glorious First of June. The young Wrens had two weeks of training as a probationer, during which time they wore navy blue overalls and could leave if they didn't like it. Colette was told she wouldn't be given the smart navy blue uniform she'd joined up to wear until the third and final week of training, once she'd committed to staying in the Wrens.

'They got us up in the morning at half past four with a klaxon and we used to have to scrub the floor of the corridor and then we would have a great big mug of tea and some bread and dripping. I thought this was fantastic. And I made friends with a girl there who came from Yorkshire as well, Sheila Tong. Anyway, eventually we were called up for an interview on what we were going to do. There were only three categories left: cooks, stewards, or Pembroke Five.'

Pembroke merely indicated it was a shore station – at that stage Wrens weren't allowed to serve on board ships – but it didn't tell them anything about what the job was. The two girls looked at each other and then at the petty officer who was advising them.

'What's Pembroke Five?'

'Can't tell you.'

'Ooh, that sounds interesting. We'll do that.'

They spent another two weeks at Mill Hill, having to wait long after everyone else on their draft had been posted away because they needed to be vetted to make sure they weren't a security risk.

'Finally the day came when we were given our uniforms. We got into a coach and off we went. I can remember Sheila saying, "Isn't this exciting. I wonder where we're going."'

About twenty minutes later they pulled into another

new Bombe base at Eastcote, just ten miles west of Mill Hill. It was a depressing anticlimax. This was the secret base? They'd been hoping for some sort of top-secret intelligence organisation hidden away and they'd ended up at a muddy building site a few miles down the road. Colette couldn't hide her disappointment.

'It looked awful. They were still building it.'

The girls were taken first into the accommodation, one of two parallel rows of large wooden huts, known as 'cabins', each housing around fifty Wrens sleeping in bunk beds. Each of these 'cabins' housed a complete shift or 'watch' of Wrens. They were built close together with water and sewage pipes running down the gap between the two rows. Each row had a central corridor linking the series of huts and at each end of each hut was a 'single cabin' for the petty officer in charge of the watch. The huts were all named after famous warships. Colette's was HMS *Orion*, after one of the ships which defeated the French at the Battle of Trafalgar, still regarded as the Royal Navy's most glorious victory. Colette was beginning to wonder if she'd made the right decision.

'Someone had said to us, this is Pembroke Five. You'll never get out of it. You'll be here 'til the end of the war, unless you drop dead. We had to put the bunks up. We had to put them together and we were scrubbing and cleaning the hut and the corridor and then finally we were taken to Block B where the Bombes were, and introduced to them.'

Pembroke Five was the unit name for all the Wrens working for Bletchley wherever they were based. The Bombes were huge, bronze machines more than six foot high, seven foot wide and two and a half foot deep (1.8m x 2.1m x 0.8m) set in rows of three, with a dozen Bombes, sometimes more, in each of the rooms or 'bays'. The new Wrens were told that they would be helping to break the German codes and that the Bombes were checking for possible settings. Each Bombe contained thirty rotating drums, every one of them replicating the action of an individual Enigma rotor. The girls had to load the drums and wire them up at the back according to instructions on the 'menu' they were given. The wires had plugs on them which Colette and the other Wrens plugged into sockets alongside the drums.

'We were shown how to plug up the back. It was very complicated, it really was. It took some learning. The drums went round at different revolutions. I can remember the noise, clackety-clackety-clackety-clack, and having your sleeves rolled up, working hard and so much stretching. They said they wanted girls not less than five foot eight inches. I was five foot eight and a half tall and even I had to stretch. It was very noisy – the clackety-clack sound. Filthy mess and stench, hot black oil dripping onto the floor.'

They worked in pairs, one of them plugging up the Bombe and the other sitting beside the Bombe at a machine designed to replicate the action of Enigma, checking the results to see if they produced German language. Colette always did the plugging up, following a 'menu' worked out at Bletchley on the basis of a piece of German text the codebreakers thought might be somewhere in a particular encoded message.

'You'd put the drums up, and then go around the back

and plug them up according to the menu. The menu was brought in to us. We had a Wren petty officer in charge of us and she would hand out the menus.'

Once it was set up, the Bombe would be switched on and go through its cycle with the drums turning round, taking just under a quarter of an hour to find the first possible setting for a string of encoded letters that would fit the menu devised by Bletchley.

'When the whole thing stopped we would take the reading from the side of the Bombe and that would go in to the girls who were doing the checking. I remember the joy of hearing the shout "job up" from the checking room, which meant that the "stop" that you'd got made sense and gave them the words they were looking for and would be bunged through on the scrambler phone to Bletchley.'

There were a lot of 'bad', stops where the checkers found the settings the Bombe had thrown up didn't work. This was usually because the little wire brushes in the back of each of the drums had got too close together and the electricity had 'shorted' across between the brushes, making a false connection.

'There were little metal brushes inside the drums and they could come together and cause a short. If it was a "bad stop" we knew there was a short somewhere and that meant we had to take all the drums out and move the brushes. We used to spend all the time while the thing was running with a pair of tweezers going over these brushes on the other drums.'

When the job was up, they always felt a bit of pride that what they were doing might have helped somehow. When they were working on an actual job they were told which of the German armed forces the code belonged to. They used codewords to identify whether it was a navy, army or air force message: porpoise for the navy, wolf for the army and eagle for the air force. When each job was finished, the chief petty officer in charge of the watch would shout, 'Job up. Strip.' As the person setting up the Bombe, it was Colette's job then to unplug the wiring and take out all of the drums as quickly as possible ready for the next menu.

'I do remember it was very hard work and there was a real sense that you were doing something important. It was a strange time, difficult to replicate really, everyone living on a knife edge. We were very well aware that we had to win the war or else. What was going to happen to us was going to be worse than anything that had been seen on the continent. There was an air of urgency about things.'

Anne Zuppinger was nineteen when she arrived at Bletchley in early 1941, in the first batch of Wrens. Her father was a corn merchant in London, a business he'd inherited from his father, a Swiss national who'd come to London in the late 1870s and married a local woman. Despite her young age, Anne was spotted early on as someone capable of carrying responsibility and earmarked as a potential officer. She understood the importance of the work and the need for total secrecy. So when Commander Denniston complained that the Wren training bases were sending them the wrong type of girls she was commissioned and sent out to the training bases to select the type of people needed by Bletchley and its outstations.

The training staff at Mill Hill, Headingley and Tullichewan made an initial selection on the basis that the Wrens sent to Bletchley had to have a good education, but they also had to be someone who wasn't going to be a security risk. They had to be dependable and prepared to do what could at times be an extremely boring job knowing that it was important to the country. They also needed to be a certain height, because the Bombe machines were quite tall, and they had to be fit and have extremely good eyesight. All this might seem easy to determine but the staff at the training bases advising the Wrens on the various jobs they could do had no idea what was going on at Bletchley, which made it difficult for them to know who would be best for the job. Anne had operated the Bombes, learning how to do it from scratch. She knew the people doing it – who was good and who was not so good. She would have a much better idea than the training staff of which Wrens to select.

'I was working with the Bombes and therefore knew exactly what was needed, whereas they had people recruiting from the various training centres who didn't know what the girls were required to do.'

Initially, Anne was just looking for people capable of working on the Bombes, but soon she was also selecting Wrens to work in the Naval Section in Hut 4 and in other roles, including working inside Hut 6. Amid concern that the Wrens were not getting the status their role deserved, all Wrens working for Bletchley whether on the Bombes or in other areas were given the intriguing job title of 'Writer Special Duties (X)'.

'When I went up to interview them, I used to try to make quite sure that the person that I was seeing would realise that this was a very vital job they were doing but also that it was going to be something that they would not be able to talk about at all.'

The extent of the secrecy at the time is difficult to imagine in today's world. Audrey Wind, from Folkestone in Kent, was only eighteen when she was picked out by Anne to operate the Bombes. A week after arriving at Tullichewan in the early summer of 1944, she and five other trainees were told to report to the administrative offices in the actual castle.

'We racked our brains to think what we had done wrong but could think of nothing.'

They were ordered to sit quietly outside the office and wait. They would be seen in alphabetical order. So the girls agreed among themselves that the first who went in would come out and tell the others what it was about.

'The first Wren was called in and we waited with bated breath for her to come out and tell us what we were there for. But when the door opened she marched straight past us and out of the castle.'

The other five wondered what on earth was going on, but as each of them went in to be briefed by Anne, they came out obeying her instructions that they must not discuss it with anyone else. Audrey was fifth to go in (there was a girl behind her whose surname was Wright). Anne told her only that there was some very secret work to do that was vitally important if they were going to win the war. She couldn't be told what the actual work was until she'd agreed to do it. In the meantime, she mustn't say anything about it to anyone else.

'I was then told "About turn" and marched out of the room, straight past poor Wren Wright.'

Anne heard about the girls' consternation later and laughed. So far as she was concerned it simply showed that she'd made the right choices when she selected those particular Wrens. They were told not to talk about it and they didn't, and all of them agreed to take the job. Anne never stopped drumming in the secrecy aspect, which was repeatedly stressed when the girls were in their various 'Wrenneries' doing the job.

'One managed to get across that this was a very vital thing and I would always tell them that it was secret work, it was something that was absolutely essential to the war effort, that it was exceedingly boring. But if they were keen to do something for the good of the country, and if that's what they'd joined up for, well then maybe this was the job for them.'

Once they arrived at the outstation and began working on the Bombes they were told that their work was vital to helping the codebreakers read the German messages. Occasionally Anne or one of the other officers would brief them on the various triumphs resulting from their work, especially if they had helped the navy.

'We had to be quite sure that their morale was kept up because it was tedious work, very tedious work, and one way was to let them know some of the intelligence that came out of the work they were doing, so that they would realise that it was an absolute priority. I know that when we finally managed to get *Bismarck*, that was one of our triumphs and they were told about that. They were also told how important it was that we knew where the submarines were in the Atlantic because our food supply was coming across the Atlantic and that was our lifeline, and so it was very vital that we should break the submarines' codes.'

Anne made sure her girls realised that while there were many brilliant people at Bletchley breaking the codes, they couldn't do it without all sorts of other people, particularly the operators intercepting the messages – some of whom were themselves Wrens – and the women operating the Bombes.

'One had many of the tremendous brains in Bletchley Park, but they relied totally on the Wrens to carry out the work they'd done and it wouldn't have been possible to break these codes unless they had Wrens operating the machines.'

The Wrens came from all walks of life, from debs to ordinary working-class girls. One of the Wrens working on Colette's watch was Lady Camilla Wallop, who went on to become a lady-in-waiting to Queen Elizabeth II but was known as plain Wren Wallop.

In their time off, Colette and her friends would read or go to the cinema, and since the food was particularly bad at Eastcote, they would visit the local NAAFI restaurant at nearby Ruislip where they could buy beans on toast for fourpence (less than 2p). When they were working days or night shifts they would go into London on the underground, queuing up in Trafalgar Square to buy cheap forces theatre tickets. Roma Davies, at the time lowly Wren Stenning, loved those trips into London from Eastcote.

'We took ourselves out for suppers, to the cinema, and even trips to the West End. It was one shilling and threepence [just over 6p] to spend the entire evening at the Variety Club watching top comedians, singers and dancers. Going into little old cafés and having beans on toast and . . . when you were in uniform people gave you things, the odd meal, or the conductor might let you have a free ride on the bus.'

London was dangerous though. When Colette and Sheila Tong were drafted to Eastcote at the end of 1943, the 'mini-Blitz' was taking place with the German air force firebombing the major cities, and the Wrens were often warned not to venture into the centre of London.

Not that they were much safer in Eastcote. One night, a German bomber dropped a 'Molotov Breadbasket', a rack containing 820 firebombs, on the 'cabin' in which Sheila and Colette were sleeping. The air-raid siren had gone off but they never went to the shelters.

'We heard an aircraft overhead. We knew it was a German aircraft. You could always tell from the "whoom, whoom, whoom" sound. All of a sudden it seemed quite low and Sheila said to me, "Let's get under the bedclothes." As if that would help! If you can't see it, you're safe!'

Suddenly there was a huge crashing noise and the Molotov Breadbasket came through the roof and destroyed the side of HMS *Orion*, hitting the water pipes that ran down between the huts.

'There was the most awful bang and a crash and wallop

and I could feel the central part of the hut was coming in. Then there was absolute silence and the sound of water pouring in. It was like one of those wartime films of ships being torpedoed with the sea rushing in.'

One of the girls broke the silence, shouting: 'Abandon ship.' There was nervous laughter from some of the girls but it shook them out of the shock and made them realise they had to move. The incendiary bombs hadn't gone off but they might at any minute. Colette grabbed her gas mask, largely because her secret store of chocolate was hidden inside its case.

'We got out of our bunks and took our service respirators and clambered out over this thing. It hadn't opened completely. Some of the bombs had burned their way out and landed somewhere else on the camp, but the rest were still there and could have gone off. We just clambered over them and got out.'

The Wrens had a four-day 'stand-off' once in every four weeks. They would work one week of days, the second week was evenings and the third week was working through the night. They came off the final night and then worked that evening from four to midnight. Then they had four days off. Most of the girls went home to see their families (and sometimes, if they were home on leave, their boyfriends) in trains that were always packed with troops.

'I used to go up to Harrogate and Sheila used to go to Hull, standing most of the time. Many's the time I've gone all the way up to Harrogate sitting in the guard's van on a bicycle.'

Colette was lucky. Her boyfriend Graham was based in

the UK so could often come up to Harrogate to see her. They'd met because he had been a pupil of Colette's aunt at St Francis Xavier's College in Liverpool.

'He came to Harrogate to see Aunt Em. She lived in Liverpool but there were terrible air raids there. Terrible. So she came to Harrogate to live with us, and that's how we got to know Graham.'

Graham Murray's father was Scottish but like Colette he had an Irish mother. He was an RAF pilot warrant officer. His job was to drop secret agents into France and other occupied countries. Here was a man who could match up to Colette's father, who had won the Military Cross on the Somme during the First World War. Graham's job was highly dangerous but he was based at RAF Tempsford in Bedfordshire, so whenever he had days off at the same time as Colette they would meet up at her parents' home.

'He was one of these chaps dropping agents. He flew Halifax aircraft and they used to have to fly at 800 feet to drop the agents and the supplies. The supplies didn't all come down by parachute, sometimes they were just dropped.'

Colette moved to Stanmore shortly before D-Day, the Allied invasion of Europe. The Wrens weren't briefed on when and where it would happen – the detail of the Allied assault had to be kept very tight among a few people who were specially briefed or, in the jargon used by those in charge, 'bigoted'. But Colette and her colleagues knew it was coming. They were banned from going on leave and on the day itself they saw the sky black with Allied bombers and knew immediately what was happening.

But while D-Day seemed to take the Allies a step closer to victory, there was bad news for Colette. Graham was reported missing while dropping supplies to resistance fighters in the Ardennes in preparation for the invasion.

'Nobody quite knew what that meant because in those days missing could mean he was a prisoner of war and that was often the case.'

There was nothing for it but to get on with the work, and even if you were in the UK you were still under threat, especially if you worked in a big city like London. The Germans responded to the D-Day invasion by firing the V1 flying bombs at London from launchers along the French and Dutch coasts. The British called the V1s doodlebugs because of the humming noise they made. The Germans fired up to a hundred a day at London and southeast England between June 1944 and March 1945. They were very frightening – silent killers. You could hear them going over and then the engine stopped and the bomb would drop wherever it cut out.

The British responded by trying to fool the Germans into thinking that they were hitting the wrong targets, so the sirens that warned of impending bombers were not used. Instead, at Stanmore there was an old man with the same type of rotating sign they used for traffic control around roadworks. Instead of saying 'Stop' on the red side of the sign and 'Go' on the green side, the sign said 'Alert' on the red side and 'All Clear' on the green.

One night Sheila and Colette were alone in the hut. There was a stand-off and most people had gone home, but it wasn't the normal four-day break, so there wasn't enough time for the two girls to go up to Yorkshire. Sheila had gone down to the washroom and Colette was getting into her bunk.

'I heard this bloody thing. Hmm. Hmm. Hmm. Hmm . . . and when it got lower and lower and louder it suddenly stopped. And I remember jumping out of my bunk and trotting down the concrete corridor in my bare feet to join Sheila, thinking to myself, I don't want to die alone. That's what I was thinking, and she was lying flat on the floor.'

Although Colette still had no word of Graham, she at least was safe and was soon moved away from the dangers of London to work on the Bombes in Hut 11 at Bletchley Park. She was quartered in a 'Wrennery' at Crawley Grange, ten miles northeast of Bletchley. The utility buses – dubbed 'liberty ships' after the boats that transport sailors from their ship and into port – took half an hour to ferry Colette and the other Wrens into work.

'We were bussed in and bussed out. We never saw any of the other people at Bletchley. We never had contact with any of them. We were completely self-contained and we did our eight hours and back to Crawley.'

Crawley Grange was a beautiful Elizabethan house which had once belonged to Thomas Wolsey, who as Lord Chancellor under Henry VIII was the second most powerful man in the country. But Wolsey fell from favour after he failed to obtain the annulment of Henry's marriage to Catherine of Aragon that would allow the King to marry Anne Boleyn, and Crawley Grange was taken away from him. Colette thought it was absolutely gorgeous.

'It had a great ballroom, panelled from the floor to the ceiling, with two bay windows, and it was haunted. The place looked perfect with the utility forces furniture in it, just right, the plain tables and things. Once a week we would go into Bedford and probably get something to eat, beans on toast or something. The rest of the time we sat in this great panelled room.'

This was their 'fo'c'sle'. Mostly they just sat and chatted, played cards or board games, or simply read, but it would have been a waste not to make full use of a beautiful ballroom and they held dances and social evenings to which they invited American or RAF airmen from the nearby bases at Molesworth and Cranfield. The Wrens who were working in the Naval Section at Bletchley also invited other members of Hut 4 to the dances. The influx of a large number of young servicewomen dramatically improved the social life for those who, like Barbara Abernethy, were lucky enough to be invited to the dances.

'All of a sudden there were lots of soldiers, Wrens and WAAFs. The Wrens used to have rather good dances. To be invited to a party at one of the Wrenneries as they were called was something to be looked forward to and enjoyed. They had very good dances.'

The Americans reciprocated and the Glenn Miller Army Air Force Band, the most popular orchestra of the time, and based just a few miles away in Bedford, frequently played at the US dances.

On one occasion, a bus-load of Wrens and Hut 4 staff were invited to a dance in a hangar at a nearby American base where Glenn Miller's band was playing. They included Adrienne Farrell, a civilian translator working in Hut 4.

'The hangar was crowded and in semi-darkness, lit only by swirling coloured spotlights and resounding with the superb but deafening noise of the band. As each of us entered we were grabbed by one of the waiting line of airmen. After the first dance, I looked eagerly round for my next partner. Alas, we were expected to stay with the same person all evening. I think my partner was as disappointed as I was. On the way home, I noticed with some puzzlement that the bus was half empty.'

Barbara Quirk, from North Cheshire, joined the Wrens in early 1943 at the age of eighteen and after a spell at Stanmore moved to Crawley Grange. She loved the countryside around the house and frequently went riding or walking across the fields.

'Crawley Grange is I think one of the most beautiful houses I have ever seen. There were fields, endless fields, and I remember one day I was walking alongside a hedge and I had my hacking jacket over my shoulder and a pheasant flew into my jacket. I was very glad when it flew away because I didn't quite know what to do with it. The fields and hedgerows were full of every shade of violet in creation, huge big lovely-smelling violets, so every Wren cabin you went into at Crawley Grange had pot after pot of beautiful violets and primroses and cowslips. Glorious, heavenly country.'

One weekend, Barbara's watch decided to hold a dance in the ballroom, but they were told by the senior officer in charge of them at the time that they couldn't have any alcohol in the grounds of Crawley Grange.

'So we got some of the men who were coming from one of the camps around – they might have been Americans, they might have been British, I can't remember now – to bring some beer. They brought a mobile bar on a jeep and parked it outside the Wrennery and when the chief officer found out, we were all gated [restricted to quarters] for a month.'

Barbara also worked on the Bombes at Bletchley. The watches ran from 8am to 4pm, from 4pm to midnight, and from midnight to 8am. The night shifts were the worst because there was often much less to do once the most common codes were broken.

'It could be a bit slower than in the daytime and some Wrens used to go and sit in the off-duty quarters and fall asleep and eventually it was said that no one was to sleep when at Bletchley so when we had a break for coffee or a roll or something we would cut the crossword out of the previous day's *Times* that was hanging up in the mansion and take it back with us and shout clues to each other from our respective Bombes.'

Colette was completely absorbed with the work and worries about Graham and many of the Wrens also had boyfriends away in the war, but there were still plenty of unattached Wrens and no shortage of young servicemen willing to attend the dances and social evenings.

'We had wonderful dances and evenings. I can remember the lawn in front of it covered in bicycles, chaps on bicycles. But somehow it wasn't that important. We were so hard at it all the time. We were kind of living for that stand-off. It was a very hard grind indeed.'

When they finished the final evening shift before the stand-off they would leave as soon as possible, taking trains packed with troops back home.

'The Admiralty were very good to us, we were the first women services to be given handbags, quite primitive shoulder bags, but an absolute boon for a woman. This was wonderful for our make-up and combs.'

They were also allowed to wear their own underwear rather than the standard long black 'apple-catcher' knickers that other servicewomen had to wear. Colette bought a remnant of beautiful, pale-blue satin during one of their trips on the bus into Bedford and took it home with her on the next stand-off so her mother could use it to make her some French knickers.

'My mother used a button to fasten them because elastic was in short supply and one time I was going home on leave and standing in the middle of the corridor as the train was packed as usual. I had to change at Kettering and I jostled to get out of the train with all my bags, stepped onto the platform, looked down and found my pale-blue satin knickers around my ankles with the platform full of American Army Air Corps. What else could I do but step out of them, put them in my pocket and ride the rest of the way home with no knickers on.'

Joan Read married her boyfriend Edward Baily in early 1942 after he joined the Royal Inniskilling Dragoon Guards, but her father was in the Royal Navy and she and her sister

Joyce decided to join the Wrens. It would be the right thing to do, they thought, and they would have a more attractive uniform than if they joined the WAAF or the ATS. Joan was twenty-one and Joyce was twenty. They were selected for 'Special Duties (X)' and followed their orders to report to the mysterious Station X with some apprehension, not having the faintest idea what they would be doing. Joan recalled that they were put to work in Hut 11 and billeted at Gayhurst Manor, which was once home to Everard Digby, one of the conspirators in the Gunpowder Plot in 1605 to blow up King James I.

'The owners of Gayhurst Manor were still in residence, Sir Walter and Lady Carlisle; occasionally we caught a glimpse of them and Lady Carlisle always had a sack tied around her waist for some unknown reason. If we were on the night watch we had to sleep during the day, of course, and I remember they had problems with an RAF aircraft flying low over Gayhurst. We found out afterwards it happened to be because my sister was sunbathing on the roof with nothing on.'

Occasionally, inevitably, one of the girls would fall pregnant, at which point a glass of milk would be put out for her each night in the galley, sparking gossip as to who it was. Once the bump began to grow they would be sent away for six months or so to have the baby before returning to the job. Sadly, unless a girl's parents looked after the baby, it was taken away and put up for adoption, a procedure that remained common for single mothers well into the 1970s.

Many of the girls were away from home, and the

watching eyes of their mothers, for the first time. But while the knowledge that their boyfriends might be sent off to die at any time induced many to go further than they would have done before the war, for others the strict moral codes of the time held sway. It had been drummed into them that 'nice girls' did not do such things until they were married. Barbara Quirk remembered that as a young Wren working in Stanmore she would go up to the West End whenever she had an evening off.

'You really worked solidly for the eight hours you were on duty but there was ample time off and we all enjoyed ourselves, it was great fun. I had a very good war, I had a ball. But you must remember in those days that there was no such thing as an overnight stay. You went and had dinner. You enjoyed yourself immensely. You might even have gone somewhere dancing and when the time came for good little Wrens to go home you shook hands and said goodbye.'

Shortly after D-Day, Anne Zuppinger got married to Alan Hill, an RAF officer she'd met at one of the dances. Clothing was rationed and she didn't have enough clothing coupons to get the material for a wedding dress. It looked as if she would be forced to get married in uniform. But Anne's bridesmaid had managed to get a wedding dress and was getting married before Anne, so she said Anne could borrow the wedding dress once she'd worn it.

'Then her wedding was put off because her husband was in the navy and he was on active service and my future husband had to arrange for our wedding to be in between operations over France, so my wedding was before hers.

So I wore her wedding dress before she wore it herself. I think that was a wonderful friendship and Wrens formed a guard of honour for us. So it really was a lovely occasion.'

Five weeks later, Alan was reported missing in operations over France, his aircraft shot down by the Germans. He'd named Anne's father as his next of kin because he didn't want her to get the fairly blunt telegram that was sent out when someone was missing.

'He was a master bomber in the Pathfinder force and the master bombers were the only ones that were sending radio messages. So they were always shot down, which I hadn't realised. I think he'd kept that to himself, so he knew that the chances of him getting through would be very slim.'

Anne's father received the telegram reporting his son-in-law missing and got in touch with Edith Blagrove, the commanding officer for all the Wrens working at Bletchley and its outstations, and she went to see Anne personally to break the bad news to her gently. Despite Alan's considerate precautions it was never going to be a happy time for Anne.

'When I heard that Superintendent Blagrove was coming to see me I pretty well knew what it would be. But I was very, very fortunate because within a couple of months he was back again, having been hidden by the underground and brought back to England.'

Alan had been back in England for some time before Anne heard the good news. He'd assumed that Anne would have been told the minute he arrived back in Britain, but because he'd come down an escape line it had to be kept secret until after he'd been debriefed. Anne couldn't be told.

'So the first I knew was when he telephoned me. I was at Steeple Claydon. He phoned the Wren officers' mess at Walton Hall and they thought they recognised his voice and told him to ring Steeple Claydon. When I answered the telephone, I was so overcome that I had to hand the telephone over to one of the other officers there to make arrangements about going to see him but it was a wonderful moment. I was one of the lucky ones. That didn't happen to all of our Wrens, of course.'

Barbara Quirk had taken her friend Pam, one of the petty officers, home and introduced her to her mother. When Barbara's brother John was killed, her mother wrote to Pam and asked her to break the news. Barbara recorded in her diary for 25 July 1944 that she had worked a day shift and returned to Crawley Grange at six o'clock in the evening.

'Pam took me outside to give me some bad news. John has been killed. There seems no point in saying any more. I don't think I really took it in. We walked round the fields and she was quite marvellous. Thank God I had her. It would have been quite unbearable alone.'

Colette had still not heard what had happened to Graham. Had he escaped like Anne's husband? Maybe he'd been captured by the Germans and was being held as a prisoner of war? The news was slow in coming through. Eventually, they heard that his aircraft had been shot down over Holland on its way back from dropping the supplies to the Resistance. Three of the crew had managed to escape down the lines. Graham wasn't one of them. He'd been too badly wounded. Pilot Warrant Officer Graham Murray was just twenty-three when he died.

'I think Mum rang me and I always remember running up the street, crying. I didn't know where I was going, what I was doing. I was distraught. It was awful really. But it was happening to all sorts of people. It took a couple of weeks but I picked myself up, dusted myself down and got on with it. But it's always stayed there. It's always there.'

5

Let's Call the
Whole Thing Off

Once the Wrens had found the settings on the Bombes for a particular Enigma code like the Red or the Brown the results were fed back to Hut 6. Jane Hughes and the other women in the Decoding Room put the settings onto the replica Enigma machines and started to type in all the messages that were in that code. The plain German text came out on strips of paper which were then stuck onto the back of the original message and passed through the wooden tunnel to the intelligence reporters in Hut 3.

Very few of the actual intelligence reporters – known as the Watch – were women, largely because there were only a few people on the night shift and Civil Service rules would not have allowed one woman to work in such close proximity to men at night in case something happened between them.

But women did take on a lot of very responsible back-room roles within Hut 3, analysing and reporting on the

German army and air force messages. The Civil Service rules might have been steeped in misogyny but so far as Mair Thomas was concerned there was no sexism at Bletchley in the way young women were treated.

'No one looked down on me or patronised me and I would say there was also equality between the sexes. There were more women than men, so the men had to watch their step. For the first time, I was judged purely on my ability and not my gender. I was paid well and had an independence I have probably not enjoyed since.'

There was a great mix of the different classes which had dominated British society as well. The debs represented a different era and the traditions they cherished would soon disappear once the war was over, while many of the young academics recruited from the universities already knew that – despite their general admiration for the Conservative Prime Minister Winston Churchill – they would be voting for Labour at the next election. Yet the issue of class never raised its head. There was an astonishing level of mutual respect which Mair felt was unique to Bletchley.

'It was a marvellous atmosphere in many ways because you weren't aware of class or background. We were there to do a job and that's all that mattered. All the differences that normally exist between people came tumbling down. There was something about the community in Bletchley Park that I haven't seen since. We were all doing the same work; sharing frustrations and confronting impossible challenges.'

Christine Brooke-Rose was just eighteen when she joined the Women's Auxiliary Air Force in 1941. She'd

had an unusual childhood. Her British father, a former
Benedictine monk and convicted thief, had married a
Swiss-American woman. So Christine was born in Geneva
and her first language was French, although the family also
spoke English and German. Christine's parents separated
when she was six and she stayed in England with her father,
but when he died in 1934 she went to live with her mother
in Brussels. In 1938, at the age of fifteen, Christine was
sent to Germany to improve her spoken German, staying
in a *Schloss* (castle) near Ulm with a baroness whose family
worshipped Hitler. A year later plans for her to go to teach
English at a school in Rosenheim, Bavaria, were only
thwarted by the outbreak of war.

Like the Wrens, the WAAF had originally been set up
during the First World War but was disbanded shortly
afterwards. It was recreated in June 1939 and from very
early on had a strict rule that all officers had to have been in
the ranks before they could be commissioned, an equality
that was unknown in any of the other services. They were
given four weeks' training and, unlike the Wrens, had their
uniforms from the very start. The training was focused on
drill, physical fitness and understanding of how the RAF
worked so that each WAAF could go on to train for the
actual job she would be doing 'without feeling awkward or
bewildered'.

Despite being fluent in German, Christine was sent to
work in the Operations Room at RAF Thornaby-on-Tees, a
coastal command station on the Yorkshire coast, where she
spent her time writing up flight records. When the station
education officer heard she spoke German he asked her

to teach the bomb disposal staff since it would help them to understand what was said on the unexploded bombs. Christine agreed but never got the chance. Now her bosses realised she spoke German so well she was not going to be wasted filling in forms for RAF Coastal Command.

'The WAAF commanding officer at Thornaby called me in. There must have been a search for people who knew German at the time. I was told I was being commissioned immediately and sent to an officer training unit at Loughborough.'

Christine was promoted to assistant section officer and called to London, to Broadway Buildings, for an interview with the head of the MI6 Air Section, Group-Captain Frederick Winterbotham, and Wing-Commander Robert Humphreys, who was in charge of air intelligence inside Hut 3. Winterbotham gave Christine a card with some highly complex German text written on it and told her to tell him what it said.

'I was asked to translate a piece of very technical German and I somehow floundered through it and I found myself in Bletchley Park as a young officer of eighteen knowing absolutely nothing.'

In fact, the only word Christine 'floundered' over was the extremely obscure *Klappenschrank*, a minor part of an army field telephone. Winterbotham was impressed. Christine was given a first-class rail warrant from Euston to Bletchley and told to report to Humphreys at the Park the very next day. When Christine arrived at Bletchley she was given a security briefing, made to sign the Official Secrets Act and shown to Hut 3, which nestled around the end of Hut 6 that was farthest away from the mansion, turning in a right-angle around and behind the codebreakers' hut. Christine walked down a narrow corridor with small offices on either side. The door to one of the offices was open, with a number of girls in civilian clothes and a teleprinter rattling away.

'I'm looking for Wing-Commander Humphreys.'

'Down the corridor and turn right.'

The corridor led past a number of rooms, one full of army officers, another containing RAF officers and civilians, then into a long, wide room with a number of women in civilian clothes working on several tables covered in long boxes containing filing cards. One large wall of the room was covered in maps of various parts of Europe, the Middle East and North Africa. Wing-Commander Humphreys was sat at one of the desks. He jumped up when he saw Christine and introduced her to his secretary Beatrice Shields, who showed her around the hut.

The first place Beatrice showed her was a square room with a large horseshoe-shaped table at which a number of men, who were called the Watch, were sat working away on pieces of paper. These were the decoded messages shoved through the hatch from Hut 6. They worked out what the message said, usually having to 'emend' it, which meant filling in gaps and correcting spellings to find the right words and make sense of the message. They then had to disguise it to make it look as if it had come from a report from a British secret agent behind enemy lines. One of the most common tricks was to say that the source had found a note or a document in a waste-paper basket in the German headquarters.

Hut 3 couldn't be honest about where the message had come from. It was vital that the Germans didn't know the British were breaking the Enigma codes, so only a very few people were allowed to know what Bletchley had achieved. Large numbers of senior officers, civil servants and politicians had no idea. The reports were sent out as if they were genuine MI6 reports from secret agents who'd managed to infiltrate German military headquarters or government offices. Christine was impressed with how clever everyone seemed to be.

'All the people in Hut 3 were people who had to emend these texts which we intercepted and would sometimes arrive in very corrupt form. You had to know German extremely well to guess what it might be. So we had some of the best German scholars there.'

The reports were sent by teleprinter to London and the other people who were 'in the know' by young women known as 'Teleprincesses'. These were usually WAAFs who operated most of the large number of teleprinters that linked Bletchley to the outside world, but some of them were civilians employed by the Foreign Office, like the first girls Christine had met when she arrived in Hut 3.

'We were all jumbled up. Nobody cared if you were in the air force or in the Foreign Office or what.'

Beatrice took Christine back to Humphreys' office and introduced her to Jean Alington, who as a shift leader in charge of the girls working on the index cards would be Christine's immediate boss.

'I was to be in the Air Index, just indexing information from the teleprints we sent up to Whitehall.'

All the intelligence reports sent out by Hut 3 were also sent to the Air Index where Jean and the other shift leaders marked up everything that needed to be recorded in pink and the rest of the shift made up the index cards or added the information to a previous card on the same subject. It could be anything from the name of a soldier or airman and what his job was to details of fuel supplies, or the routes and timings of rail or naval convoys. One of the things Christine had to note down on the cards was the repeated references to the new secret weapon being developed at Peenemünde in northern Germany – this would turn out to be the V1 flying bombs, the doodlebugs. It was worrying for her at times to think of how many secrets she and her colleagues were trusted to keep.

'I remember being so frightened. I was so young, I had no experience of any kind and I was so frightened of saying something by mistake off-duty that I stopped reading the newspapers altogether and stopped listening to the wireless because then I would know that everything I knew was secret that I had read that day in messages.'

The period when Christine arrived at Bletchley also saw the arrival of a group of people who would change the lives of a number of the women, including both Christine and Barbara Abernethy. Barbara was now in charge of Commander Denniston's office and in early 1941 he said he needed her to stay late that night.

'Commander Denniston said he had something important to tell me. "There are going to be four Americans who are coming to see me at twelve o'clock tonight," he said. "I require you to come in with the sherry. You are not to tell anybody who they are or what they will be doing."'

The Japanese attack on Pearl Harbor that would bring the Americans into the war was still ten months away but already the British and American codebreakers were preparing to work together to share their resources and abilities to break the German, Italian and Japanese codes. Waiting outside for her boss's signal to come in, Barbara tried to work out how she was supposed to manhandle the cask of sherry into his office on her own.

'It came from the Army and Navy Stores and was in a great big cask which I could hardly lift. But Commander Denniston rang the bell and I struggled in and somehow managed to pour glasses of sherry for these poor Americans.'

It was something of an amazing experience for Barbara. The work she'd been involved in both at Broadway Buildings and at Bletchley was top secret, but this was somehow even more momentous. Despite having worked for the Code and Cypher School for nearly four years, she was still only nineteen. It felt as if she was taking part in something extraordinary. She couldn't take her eyes off the American officers.

'I'd never seen Americans before, except in the films. I just plied them with sherry. I hadn't the faintest idea what they were doing there, I wasn't told. But it was very exciting and hushed voices. I couldn't hear anything of what was said but I was told not to tell anybody about it. I guess it wasn't general knowledge that the Americans had got any liaison with Bletchley. It was before Pearl Harbor, you see, and presumably President Roosevelt wasn't telling everybody there was going to be any liaison at that stage.'

Once the Americans entered the war in December 1941, the first of what would be several hundred codebreakers from the US Navy and the US Army began arriving at Bletchley. There was a mixed reception, with some of Christine's colleagues in Hut 3 very wary of the Americans. Jean Alington couldn't hide her distrust.

'I remember with horror the American invasion when every section had an American. We believed they had no sense of security and were terrified that material they took out of the Hut would go astray. We felt strongly that they would never have come into the war but for Pearl Harbor.'

That attitude was common and not really surprising. Britain had been fighting with its back against the wall. The Americans had provided immense help with vital supplies and financial backing but there was still resentment at the way in which they'd dragged their feet while the Nazis rampaged across Europe. Britain was weighed down by two years of war, the Americans seemed to act as if they owned the place, and Jean was wrongly convinced they weren't going to be capable of pulling their weight.

'They were different animals, and the English they spoke had different meanings. They were fat, we were emaciated. They were smart (eleven different sorts of uniform), we were almost in rags. They were rich, we were poor. They brought in alcohol: "Have a rye, sister." "We don't drink here." We were overworked and exhausted, and having to teach people who barely knew where Europe was, was the last straw.'

Pamela Draughn was in charge of a shift in the Duddery in Hut 6, using captured Enigma machines to try to work out what was wrong with 'dud' messages, messages that wouldn't decode properly using the Enigma settings that the Hut 6 codebreakers had worked out for that particular radio network. Some of the more junior Americans were allocated to her shift.

'The Americans were all very nice. They were very anxious to please. The ones I got, there were half a dozen, some from state university, nothing like as intelligent as our graduates, and two from Princeton and Harvard, both very intelligent.'

But as with the then popular song 'Let's Call the Whole Thing Off', sung by Fred Astaire and Ginger Rogers, the two sides found themselves divided by a single language.

'The second day they were there I said to the one who was most intelligent: "What happened to Theo today, Teddy?" and Teddy said: "Aw gosh, the heck, Pam. He's been shot." I was absolutely horrified. What sort of country was this that could shoot people just like that, and I looked at him for a bit and then I said: "What for?" And he said: "Oh you know, all these illnesses we're supposed to get when we go to Europe." He meant he'd been inoculated and I quite seriously thought he'd been shot.'

The mutual misunderstandings came to a head in the summer of 1942, during the 4 July Independence Day celebrations, when the Americans challenged the 'Brits' to a game of rounders. Barbara organised it but the Americans turned out to have a limited understanding of the rules of the game.

'They nearly went home. Now in the United States, where you play baseball, you don't need to get all the way home in one go to score. As long as you get all the way home eventually you score. Now our rules for rounders, of course, were very tough. You had to go all the way round in one go.'

If you didn't go round in one go, you didn't score a 'rounder'. It was impossible for the Americans to grasp the idea that you had to go right round the circuit to score a single run so they assumed that Barbara's explanation of the rules couldn't be right.

'It was a lovely day, we all played well, and at the end of the game we all sort of clapped each other on the back and the Americans said: "Well, we're sorry we beat you," and the British captain said: "I'm sorry, but we beat you." The Americans were a little touchy. They were convinced that they'd won and it took a bit of explanation on somebody's part to soothe ruffled feathers. It all ended with drinks all round; actually we agreed we'd won by our rules and they'd won by their rules. So that was all right. But they never asked us to play again.'

Despite Jean's doubts, and the arguments over the rules for rounders, the working relationship between the British and American codebreakers was exceptionally close. The leading US experts were the equals of their British counterparts and both sides pulled their weight. There was a very good bond between the two sides throughout the war.

Christine spent her time off preparing for the post-war era. She was very conscious of the fact that the people she was working with were far better educated than she was and she was determined to go to university. So she was studying for her Higher School Certificate in English, History, Latin and French.

'I called it my first university because I arrived there so ignorant, so uneducated, and there I was thrown in with all these toffs and scholars and so on. I didn't know as much about literature and other things as I later came to know or as the people around me knew. They were all interested in the things that I wanted to know about.'

The Bletchley Park Club ran an increasing number of sections and many of Christine's new colleagues took part, particularly in the chess and music sections. Christine's supervisor Jean Alington had been a member of the D'Oyly Carte Opera Company before the war but she was by no means alone in her abilities. The number of top musicians joining the Park was staggering. Jean was part of a lively opera group run by James Robertson, later musical director of Sadler's Wells; the standard of the choir had improved dramatically since Jane Hughes and Diana Russell-Clarke first joined it and it was now conducted by Sergeant Herbert Murrill, future head of music at the BBC. Another future BBC musician was the bassoonist Michael Whewell, who would go on to take charge of the BBC Symphony Orchestra. The many professional musicians included the Welsh composer Daniel Jones, the violinist Ludovic Stewart, and the singers Jill Medway and Douglas Craig (then known as Douglas Jones), who was subsequently the company manager at Glyndebourne.

James Robertson was also the choirmaster in the local church. Ann Lavell and Julie Lydekker, two of the WAAFs working in the main Air Section, were members of his choir.

'There was a little church just behind the Park and they did a little Sunday service for the workers and Julie and I sang in that. James Robertson was a really well-known conductor, so it was quite an excitement being in his choir.'

Christine was too busy studying at this point to take much notice. She would cycle in from her billet with a textbook open on the basket in front of her, sat reading textbooks on her breaks, and was forever walking into Hut 3 with her head in a book.

'I didn't have a great social life because I was working for Oxford and Cambridge entrance. I was still worried about my education. I had to stop in the end because life was too difficult with shift work and so on.'

The pace of the war was hotting up. During 1942, British soldiers were fighting huge battles across the deserts of North Africa where the German General Erwin Rommel, known as the Desert Fox, had pushed them back to the Egyptian border. Hut 6 and Hut 3 were working hard to produce the intelligence needed to help regain the lost ground. Shortly after General Bernard Montgomery took charge of the British 8th Army, the so-called Desert Rats, Bletchley decoded the message that turned the tide. Rommel sent a long report to Hitler explaining what he planned to do next; it was encoded using the Red Enigma and read almost immediately in Hut 6.

But it wasn't the only important message the code-breakers were reading. Hut 6 had broken the German Air Force Enigma code used by the aircraft escorting Rommel's supply ships across the Mediterranean and the Naval Section in Hut 4 was reading the main Italian naval codes, which also carried details of the supply convoys. This allowed the Royal Navy and the RAF to intercept the German supply convoys and sink them, leaving Rommel without the fuel and the spare parts he needed to keep his tanks moving across the desert.

Montgomery knew Rommel's plans and he knew Rommel's weaknesses, ensuring a series of victories first at Alam Halfa, then at El Alamein, the British Army's first real victory of the war, achieved with a great deal of assistance from Bletchley Park. Those left behind in Britain had something to cheer. Nobody in Hut 3 minded when Montgomery claimed the victory was the result of his tactical brilliance and grabbed the glory. Everyone knew they had to keep the Enigma secret, and anyway it was the soldiers at the front line who were doing the difficult, dangerous stuff. But there was an 'explosion of fury' in the Watch when Montgomery ignored Hut 3's subsequent reports showing that Rommel's forces were on their knees with only eleven tanks able to move. Montgomery sat still rather than go in for the kill. Lives would be lost as a result, and it wasn't the only time it would happen. Throughout the war, there were irritating moments when naval, army or air force commanders ignored the codebreakers' intelligence at their cost. Nevertheless, the stranglehold the British now had on Rommel's supply of fuel, parts and food – thanks to Bletchley Park and the intelligence on his plans – ensured that the Germans were driven out of North Africa.

Christine had impressed in the Air Index where her research had produced a huge chart detailing every major German unit and its location, which Jean pinned to the wall. All the intelligence reporters consulted it. Christine was developing a good reputation as a useful intelligence analyst and was moved to a new section liaising between the Hut 3 Air and Military Sections.

'We had to analyse the German messages and try to work out a priority list for the cryptographers in Hut 6 and for the intercept stations, which frequencies to concentrate on and which keys to try to break first. That was much more interesting.'

Jean also moved to the new section, which was located behind a map partition in Hut 3 and called 3L. It examined all of the material coming into the hut to decide which Enigma codes and which frequencies were the most productive and so needed to take priority. It was a role that Jean enjoyed because of the increased responsibility it gave her.

'It was a cold winter, so we were warmed by a paraffin stove, which was kicked over. The ensuing flames nearly put an end to us, our venture and the whole hut. We built a door to keep others out and George Crawford wrote above it in Greek, "Let no one enter here who is not primarily interested in mathematics."'

There were blackboards on the walls on which Christine drew the network diagrams of the radio networks that were the most important priority. They called the network diagrams 'Stars' because the control station was drawn in the middle with the other radio stations located around and linked to it by straight lines, making the diagram look like a star. The aim for Jean was to ensure maximum efficiency in terms of intercepting and decoding the most important messages.

'We were sent into Hut 6 to familiarise ourselves with the machines working there, we liaised with the traffic analysis log readers; we also made time and study assessments of how to speed up the flow of decodes to the Watch. We tried to get better conditions for personnel working in appalling discomfort and became agony aunts for the miserable and uncomfortable.'

The section was dominated by women: Jean, Christine and Leslie Tyrell, who read every Enigma message that passed through Hut 3, grading them according to importance.

'We each prepared a weekly news sheet for Mr Churchill on the areas we were covering. We swapped areas frequently so that we should be competent in all of them.'

Christine was soon made the chief liaison officer with the Fusion Room, which looked at all the raw material, gathering intelligence from the intercepted plain-language conversations between the enemy operators, tracking their locations and finding information that would help make sense of the decoded messages. Christine might have thought she wasn't clever enough. Her superiors clearly didn't agree.

'I was promoted quite quickly, I was flight officer quite soon. I felt a sense of responsibility, but at the same time that there was a great gap between what I felt I really was, which was totally ignorant, and what was needed to do this exciting job, and it really was very exciting.'

Rodney Bax, an Intelligence Corps captain working in the Fusion Room, began chatting to Christine. He'd studied at the Royal School of Music before the war and wanted to become a composer. He was 'tall and straight', paid her a lot of attention and they went out on dates to the cinema. The relationship appeared to blossom, although Christine wasn't at all sure she wanted it to go anywhere.

The numbers of people coming into Bletchley were rising rapidly, with more than five thousand people working there in August 1943 compared to the hundred or so who had first arrived outside the mansion four years earlier in August 1939. The wooden huts were too small to house so many staff and Hut 3 and Hut 6 moved into a new purpose-built concrete and brick building known as Block D; they confusingly kept their hut names. It was safer to continue to call them Hut 3 and Hut 6 than come up with a name that might give away the fact that Bletchley had broken the Enigma codes. Rodney had now been attached as Fusion Room liaison officer on the Hut 3 Watch. Christine's relationship with him was getting very close, and Rodney seemed infatuated. He had even devised his own 'secret signal' to remind her he was there. As he walked past her office, he would whistle a piece of music by Mozart.

The numbers of staff at Bletchley were now far too large to be housed in billets and Ann Lavell was one of a large number of WAAFs who were moved into a new camp built behind the mansion on Church Green. There were a lot of very basic Nissen huts, with round corrugated-iron roofs.

'We were hauled out of our billets, many of us wailing and screaming mightily, and by this time we were all dressed up as flight sergeants. A flight sergeant is really quite somebody in an ordinary RAF station but we were nobodies. We were put into these frightful huts that took about twenty-four people and had these dangerous cast-iron stoves in them that got red hot and sent out smoke everywhere.'

A similar barracks was built for the soldiers, including the army's female service, the ATS, at Shenley Road, also behind the Park. There were major problems because the officers running the new camps didn't understand the unique atmosphere at Bletchley, which Ann believed was a key factor in why the codebreakers were so successful.

'You did have this rather happy atmosphere of tolerance. Very eccentric behaviour was accepted fairly affectionately and I think people worked and lived there who couldn't possibly have worked and lived anywhere else. People who would obviously have been very, very ill at ease in a normal air force camp with its very strict modes of behaviour and discipline were very happy, very at ease in Bletchley.'

The camp authorities couldn't understand why the girls were not subject to normal military discipline. They also resented the fact that they had so little control over them and no idea what they were doing once they crossed into Bletchley Park itself.

'There was a terrible feeling between the camp authorities and the Bletchley Park people. They couldn't bear it because they didn't know what we did and because we could get in past the sentries. The guards actually said: "Halt, who goes there?" If you arrived at night, they did the bit about "friend or foe" and you said "friend" and they said "advance, friend, and be recognised". The camp people absolutely hated not knowing what was going on and some of the officers tried to bully out of the junior people what they were doing.'

Barbara Mulligan was one of the WAAF teleprinter and wireless operators communicating with the people on the front line who needed the intelligence. She remembered the huts on the Church Green camp as being very basic, and freezing cold in winter, a problem that wasn't helped by the inadequate heating and the fact that WAAF rules insisted that one window always had to be open. But they were young. The country was at war. They just got on with it.

'There were dozens of huts and we were in Hut 59. No toilets. There were special toilet huts, quite a long way from the huts. If you wanted the toilet, you had to march across a field. Finding your way in the middle of the night wasn't funny. One particular night I tripped over a couple. We just accepted it.'

The girls spent a lot of their time with the other people in the hut in which they lived, not all of whom worked in the same part of Bletchley Park as they did. Barbara and the other girls read, knitted or just chatted.

'When we only had a couple of hours spare we would just have a gossip or queue up to have a bath because you were only allowed a couple a week. It was like one big family, just a couple of dozen girls in one big hut on these funny beds. Three biscuits they called them. A mattress, a couple of sheets and a blanket and that was it and we just accepted it – that was war.'

Between a series of shifts they had two days off and Barbara would never stay on camp. Usually she'd meet up in London with her sister Gill, who was also in the WAAF and based the other side of London.

'We met up in Euston all the time and I was waiting in Euston Station for Gill and a woman came up to me and said, "Get off my pitch!" Needless to say, I did. We'd get up very early so that we could go to Lyons Corner House for breakfast and in those days a lot of big organisations would give free seats to people and we went to the opera for the very first time – free.'

Once the US Air Force base at Bedford heard there were a lot of young servicewomen at Bletchley Park, they started inviting them to their dances, sending an open-backed army truck to pick them up.

'So every Saturday night, anybody who was off-duty would be taken over to Bedford and we would be allowed to dance with the men or have a drink and go to their canteen. We all had American friends, of course, and it was great fun. (I had been engaged but my fiancé had been shot down.) They would take us in a lorry and the lorry would bring us back; elegant travel – standing in the back of a big lorry.'

Unlike Christine, Barbara Mulligan and the other girls who worked with her had no real idea of what they were doing. They certainly didn't know that Bletchley Park had broken top German codes like Enigma and they only had a hazy idea of what effect their work might be having on the war.

'We knew it was all hush-hush, and somehow it was impressed upon us that we must keep our mouths shut so I never talked to anybody about anything. I never even told my family what I was doing. Every now and then we were told that we were anticipating or were taking part in some big push that led to a battle but that was all we ever knew. We knew that we were doing good work and that was great.'

In May 1943, the US Army sent some officers to work in Hut 3. Most of them were chosen by Jim Rose who'd been sent to Washington to interview potential candidates, but the first one was a young American lawyer, Lieutenant-Colonel Telford Taylor. Christine had to introduce him to the work that was done on the indexes and in her own section.

'Telford had first arrived on his own and I was detailed to explain things to him. It was quite an odd experience because he was much too high-up to be interested in this kind of routine work.'

With the strains of the job making it impossible to keep up her studies, Christine began to take more interest in the social activities at Bletchley. Bill Marchant, the deputy head of Hut 3, ran the annual Christmas revues, so it was hard for members of Hut 3 not to become involved in some way, even if it was only as supporters, and Christine loved them.

'There were a lot of people with talent there who wrote bits and there were a few actors doing their bit for the war

and a lot of amateurs. It was like a university revue, like
Footlights. We thought they were splendid. I've no idea if
they really were. The performances may not have been so
great but I think the scripts were fairly good because there
were a lot of very bright people there.'

Musical performances, plays and films took place in
the assembly hall on a regular basis and with so many
professional musicians around there were frequent trips
to see performances in the West End.

'We would go up to London to see a play or a concert.
There were people like Peter Calvocoressi who would
give musical evenings in their billets. I remember Bryn
Newton-John, an RAF officer in Hut 3 whose daughter
Olivia became a well-known pop star, would sing German
Lieder. People went cycling around the countryside and
there were a lot of love affairs going on.'

Rodney Bax and Christine soon became engaged,
although she was unclear how this had happened and
felt as if she was being rushed towards marriage by both
Rodney and her mother. An attempt to break off the
engagement failed and she and Rodney were married in
Kensington in early 1944, not long after her twenty-first
birthday. A brief honeymoon in the Scilly Isles did nothing
to reassure Christine that she'd made the right decision,
but she just got on with it.

The arrival of the Americans had added to the social
life with their penchant for hard drinking, particularly of
whisky and other spirits. Christine found it hard to believe
that they could drink so much and yet seemed to stay
relatively sober.

'It was astonishing. I don't know if it was just the war or me being terribly innocent. I remember my husband and I being invited to dinner at the local hotel in Leighton Buzzard where all the Americans were billeted, and after dinner, all the Americans, each one, would order another whisky and another Drambuie and another round. It was absolutely amazing and we had to cycle back to the billet where we were living and I remember being really very zigzaggy. It wasn't that they were alcoholics. It was just the war atmosphere. They did drink far more. That was the American culture.'

Telford Taylor was in the office across the corridor from Christine's and with the Americans classified as an independent US unit he was able to obtain unlimited supplies of coffee and sugar. With sugar rationed and real coffee virtually unavailable in wartime Britain, it was only natural that Taylor would share these riches with the pretty girl in the office across the corridor from his own.

'He was in charge of the American Liaison Section, which was just opposite where we were in Hut 3, so they would all come in for coffee and I knew them quite well. He was very handsome, he looked like the film star Gary Cooper, and he was a very interesting person.'

Christine was in an unhappy marriage; Telford Taylor was away from his wife and family for the duration. When Rodney was taken into hospital with pneumonia, what followed seemed inevitable. Christine and Telford began an affair, spending time in hotels in London to avoid any gossip in Bletchley. Christine was sanguine about the affair. She expected no more of it than she expected of her marriage.

'It was just one of those things. I was twenty-two and he was in his late thirties. I don't know how these things happened. He had quite a good sense of humour. He was a nice man, a lawyer. He liked to tell me all about the American law system. But he was very musical.'

When Rodney came out of hospital, Christine told him about the affair.

'He was very, very British and he and Telford talked together. Telford was terribly amused afterwards because he thought my husband was so British, shaking hands and saying that everything was all right, which of course it wasn't. It just made him laugh because Americans don't face things the way gentlemen used to.'

Rodney clearly hoped that Christine's affair with Telford was a passing infatuation and would all blow over, and even though Christine knew he was probably right, she also knew that her marriage to Rodney was not going to work either. After a miserable and very lonely first Christmas together as man and wife, she finally made the break and told Rodney it was over.

6

Turing and the U-boats

Phoebe Senyard spent the first week or so of April 1940 cramming files into cupboards and squeezing the desks in Hut 4 even closer together to make space for Alan Turing to attempt to break the German Navy's Enigma codes. No one believed that even he could do this. The main German naval Enigma, codenamed Dolphin, was far more complex than the German army and air force codes they were breaking in Hut 6. But Mr Turing was determined to do it, although from what he said that was only because 'no one else was doing anything about it and I could have it to myself'.

It didn't seem a very sensible reason to waste time trying to break an unbreakable code – the Dolphin Enigma had a choice of three out of eight rotors instead of the three out of five on the army and air force Enigmas and used much more complex settings – but the German U-boats were attacking the British ships bringing supplies of oil, machinery and food across the Atlantic. Britain depended on those supplies. If the new section succeeded it would help the supply convoys to avoid the U-boats, more supplies would get through and that would help win the war. So Phoebe set about reorganising the office yet again.

'We put our backs into it in order to welcome the newcomers, by tidying up our files and papers, binding and storing into cupboards all signals and books not in current use. Everyone who could be spared temporarily from their jobs was pressed into service and room was made for it, but it was a tight squeeze. We almost felt as if we ought to all breathe in together.'

It was tight but it was worth it. No sooner had Alan Turing and his friend and fellow mathematician Peter Twinn moved in than they received two important 'pinches'. A German U-boat was trapped and sunk while trying to lay mines in the Firth of Clyde and two of the rotors for the Dolphin Enigma were recovered. More importantly, the German naval patrol boat *Schiff 26* was captured and coding documents found on board showed how the system worked.

Now they had a real chance of breaking the Dolphin Enigma, Messrs Turing and Twinn were given their own offices in Hut 8. They'd been part of the pioneering three-man team helping Dilly Knox to break Enigma, brilliant minds but not very good at organising themselves. They were untidy and kept losing things. It worried Frank Birch, head of the German Naval Section.

Alan Turing was widely regarded as eccentric, largely because he just thought at a different level to most people. He had difficulty dealing with most women and often spoke very fast, more out of enthusiasm than anything else, giving people the false idea that he had a stutter. He cycled into work wearing a gas mask to stop the pollen sparking off his hay fever, chained his coffee mug to a radiator and converted his life savings into silver bars as insurance against a collapse of the pound caused by the costs of the war. Having persuaded his bank, with a great deal of difficulty, to get him the silver bars, he buried them, working out an elaborate set of instructions so he could find them once the war was over and the danger to the currency had passed. But he never did find them again.

Frank Birch knew that Alan Turing was the right person to lead the attempts to break the Dolphin Enigma but he also knew he was the wrong person to run the actual hut. He and Peter Twinn had been given another codebreaker, Tony Kendrick, the other member of Dilly's original team, so he was someone they were very comfortable working with. Mr Kendrick, who was badly crippled as a result of having polio as a child, had been head boy at Eton and was a brilliant codebreaker in his own right. Another codebreaker was due to arrive shortly. What they really needed now they had their own offices were their own equivalents of Phoebe to make sure everything was organised properly.

Pat Wright came from a working-class family in Woolwich, on the border between southeast London and Kent. Pat, the daughter of a machine-fitter, was seventeen and had just left school. She was on a secretarial course when she received a letter out of the blue telling her to report to the Foreign Office in London.

'I was just approaching my eighteenth birthday. I had a letter asking if I would go for an interview at the Foreign

Office. There were several other girls there. They told us they wanted us to do something but they couldn't tell us what it was and that we'd be hearing from them. So I went home and my mother said: "What did they want you for?" and I replied: "I haven't the faintest idea."'

Eventually another letter arrived, this time with a train pass to go to Bletchley. Other girls from the secretarial college were going too. They took the train from Euston to Bletchley and were picked up at the station and taken up to the mansion, where they were lectured by 'a very ferocious-looking security officer' and made to sign the Official Secrets Act.

'It was then read out to us in no uncertain terms that on no account were we to tell anybody what we were doing. Nor were we to say we were on secret work. It wasn't secret. We were the evacuated office of the Foreign Office and we were copy typists.'

They were then told what they would actually be doing. It was very secret. They would be decoding messages.

'Well everybody knows the Foreign Office has codes. It didn't seem very secret. We trailed over to Hut 8 where they said: "Well, the thing is, it's German naval codes, we've broken the codes and we want you to do the decoding" – collapse of several young ladies in a heap. None of us were fluent German speakers.'

Once in Hut 8, which still looked quite bare, they were shown into a big room. It seemed the obvious description of the room, so from then on that became the name of the office in which the girls worked – the Big Room.

'It was explained to us that the German codes had been

broken by this super machine that had been invented. At the same time every day, the Germans transmitted this weather message beginning exactly the same way. This was, of course, not anything that we lesser mortals had to worry about. This was the brainy boys' department.'

The Big Room had a number of modified Typex machines in it which, like those in the Hut 6 Decoding Room, were designed to work just like the Enigma machine.

'There were three wheels out of a box of eight which were put into the machine and then turned to the right letter of the alphabet, and then there was a plugboard with plug leads that went everywhere. You started off typing and then with a bit of luck you suddenly saw something you could recognise as German.'

It was hard, tiring work, and surprisingly messy. The keys on the modified Typex machines were very stiff and had to be pressed down very hard and sprang back up with a loud clunk.

'Anybody who works a computer now that has this light touch would be horrified. It was very, very noisy. We had to grease the wheels of the machine from a big tub of Vaseline and it got all over your clothes, so by the end of the day they looked a bit tatty.'

The machines printed the text of the German messages onto a long strip of sticky tape which they cut into lengths of half a dozen words and stuck to the back of the original message. It was passed to the Naval Section in Hut 4, carried across the Park by messengers who reported to Phoebe.

*

The new codebreaker was a bit of a surprise – a young woman a week off her twenty-third birthday and straight out of university. At this stage all the codebreakers devising ways to break Enigma, both in Hut 8 and in the Hut 6 Machine Room, were men.

Joan Clarke was the daughter of a Church of England clergyman. She was born and brought up in West Norwood, south London, where she went to Dulwich High School before obtaining a place at Newnham College, Cambridge, to study mathematics. She'd been recruited earlier that year by Gordon Welchman, who'd been one of her tutors, and had agreed to join Hut 6 once she'd completed her degree course.

She didn't know her results at this stage but she would take a double first, as Mr Welchman knew she would. She'd done all the work, got far better marks than many of her male contemporaries at Cambridge, but she wouldn't be awarded an actual degree because, while Cambridge allowed women to study at the women's colleges of Girton and Newnham and take exactly the same exams as the men who were reading the same subjects, it did not award degrees to women, and would not do so until 1961.

'I arrived at Bletchley Park on 17 June and after the routine administrative matters I was collected by Alan Turing to work on naval Enigma in Hut 8, instead of with Welchman in Hut 6, because of the documents taken from the German patrol boat.'

Messrs Turing, Twinn and Kendrick were known as 'the Seniors' by the rest of Hut 8 and Joan officially became the first female 'Senior' a few days after she arrived when

Turing had an additional table placed in 'the Seniors' Room' just for her.

'I think it was Kendrick who said, "Welcome to the Sahibs' Room" – the only time that I met that term for it. Kendrick, exceptionally, never progressed beyond calling me Miss Clarke, and himself was known only by his surname. Another exception to the general use of Christian names was Turing, but this was not because of any need of formality with the head of Hut 8; he was widely known by his nickname, Prof, even during the short time when an actual university professor was working with us.'

After a 'sketchy' introduction from Alan Turing, who was not very good at explaining things, largely because he found it difficult to relate to people who didn't know things that he took for granted, Joan was set to work using the documents found on board the *Schiff 26* to find a way into the Dolphin Enigma. She was put on night shifts very quickly. Civil Service regulations about men and women working together on nights didn't apply to Seniors. There was only one person on a night shift in the Seniors' Room.

The captured documents enabled them to break the Dolphin Enigma messages for six days from April but the information wasn't enough to break them on a daily basis. It proved they could be broken and it gave them a good idea of how to do it but it wasn't enough.

The occupation of France had given the Germans new submarine bases on the western French coast, which made it much easier for them to attack the Allied convoys crossing the Atlantic. Meanwhile, the Germans were doing their own codebreaking. They'd broken the British

Merchant Navy code so they could read all the convoys' messages and knew the precise routes they were taking. The German U-boats operated in 'wolf packs'. They lined up from north to south across the shipping routes. Once one of the U-boats spotted an Allied convoy it would shadow it, sending out homing signals to draw in the other members of the pack. When all the U-boats were assembled, they would pounce en masse.

The Admiralty's Operational Intelligence Centre needed Bletchley to tell them where the U-boats were so they could route the Atlantic convoys around the wolf packs, but Hut 8 couldn't get anywhere near breaking the codes used on a regular basis. They desperately needed more pinches.

Ian Fleming, who after the war would go on to write the James Bond books, worked in naval intelligence, liaising with MI6 and Bletchley Park. He dreamed up what his boss Admiral John Godfrey, the Director of Naval Intelligence, described as a 'cunning scheme' to try to obtain a German naval Enigma machine with all of its rotors and settings.

Ian Fleming's elaborate plan to get the 'pinch' from a German ship required a captured German bomber. 'I suggest we obtain the loot by the following means,' he wrote before outlining a plan that had all the feel of a first, tentative blueprint for the fictional hero who was to make him famous. Those taking part in Operation Ruthless should each be 'tough, a bachelor, able to swim', he wrote, pencilling in his own name in brackets alongside one of the positions. 'Pick a tough crew of five, including a pilot, wireless operator and word-perfect German speaker

(Fleming). Dress them in German Air Force uniform, add blood and bandages to suit.'

They would wait until the next German air raid on London and, as the bombers returned home, take off and hide among the other aircraft. On the French side of the Channel the bomber would send out an SOS. It would then switch off one engine, lose height fast, 'with smoke pouring from a candle in the tail', and ditch in the sea. The team would then put off in a rubber dinghy, having ensured that the bomber sank before the Germans could identify it, and wait to be rescued by the German Navy. Fleming's plan continued: 'Once aboard rescue boat, shoot German crew, dump overboard, bring boat back to English port.'

Frank Birch thought it was a 'very ingenious plot' and gave it Bletchley's backing. But Operation Ruthless was called off, causing immense disappointment at Bletchley Park. 'Turing and Twinn came to me like undertakers cheated of a nice corpse yesterday, all in a stew about the cancellation of Ruthless,' Birch told Fleming. 'The burden of their song was the importance of a pinch. Did the authorities realise that there was very little hope, if any, of their deciphering current, or even approximately current, Enigma for months and months and months – if ever – without a pinch.'

During this period there was not much for the girls to do but sit and wait. There were very few messages being broken and none of them were broken until sometime after they had been transmitted. Pat Wright spent a lot of time sitting by the lake thinking, but she rarely spoke to any of the people from the other huts.

'The lake was a place you went for peace and quiet. There was a landing stage there and a boat and you didn't think anything of it if when you were coming off shift at midnight you saw a young man in the boat in the middle of the lake. They were just taking time to think.'

Pat was billeted in Bletchley itself, a short ten-minute walk away from the Park. Bletchley was an important railway junction and there were a lot of railway employees in the town. Len Tomlin was an engine driver and his wife Nessa, who was in her forties, was not one to mince her words, as Pat soon found out.

'She was a very capable woman with a range of language I had never encountered before. I had been brought up fairly strictly and she used words I hardly knew the meaning of. I remember it was the first house I had come across that had a toilet in the garden and I spent five minutes of my first evening there with my toilet bag touring around looking for the bathroom. But Mrs Tomlin was very good to me. She had an engine driver husband and a fireman son and she never took the tablecloth off. She always had food on the table.'

In her time off, Pat would meet up with other girls from Hut 8 and sit in the buffet at the station. If she had more than a day off at a time she would go home to Woolwich to see her parents. They were curious as to what she did but her father clearly knew better than to ask and when her mother asked why she worked so many nights she told her it was because of the wartime shortage of typewriters. She had to work nights to get access to a typewriter.

With the U-boats sinking several hundred Allied ships

between June and October 1940, Hut 8 came under increasing pressure to break the Dolphin Enigma. It wasn't until the early spring of 1941 that they began to see the light. The first of a series of pinches of Enigma key tables that would turn the tide was obtained in a commando raid on a German armed trawler, the *Krebs*, off the Norwegian Lofoten Islands in March. This allowed Bletchley to break some old messages but nothing new that would have provided useful intelligence. Pat Wright remembered it as a very quiet, boring time. If nothing was happening, she and the other girls in the Big Room tended to mess about a bit just to liven things up and keep themselves amused.

'With three or four teenagers in the same room things could sometimes get a bit silly. The Seniors didn't really know how to cope with four girls lying on their backs kicking their arms and legs in the air like overturned beetles.'

It was during this frustrating period of occasional breaks that Alan Turing and Joan Clarke began going out together to the cinema or for the occasional drink. They enjoyed each other's company and Joan seems to have been the first woman outside of his immediate family with whom he was able to make a connection.

'Turing wrote an account – Prof's Book – of Enigma Theory and methods which were still largely new to me. I was the guinea pig to test whether his explanation and examples were understandable.'

She realised that their relationship was different to the one he had with the male codebreakers but she was pleasantly surprised when he revealed quite how different their relationship was.

'I suppose that the fact that I was a woman made me different. We did do some things together, perhaps went to the cinema and so on. But certainly it was a surprise to me when he said; I think his words probably were: "Will you consider marrying me?" But although it was a surprise I really didn't hesitate in saying yes, and then he leaned by my chair and kissed me, though we didn't have much physical contact.'

The following day, Alan Turing told her about an issue that was troubling him. It didn't affect his feelings for her, but she needed to know about it.

'I suppose we went for a bit of a walk together after lunch. He told me that he had this homosexual tendency and naturally that worried me a bit because I did know that was something that was almost certainly permanent, but we carried on.'

Alan Turing told Shaun Wylie, an old friend from Cambridge who had joined the Seniors' Room, that he and Joan were engaged, but no one else in the hut knew and Joan didn't wear a ring. At any event, there were soon other causes for celebration. The pattern in the key tables captured in the Lofoten raid allowed them to work out the entire set of keys and Harry Hinsley found a reliable source of cribs in weather reports broadcast to the U-boats. He also realised that the weather ships that sent out the reports would need to have the same Enigma codes but would be much more vulnerable to capture than a warship.

A series of raids followed in which two German weather ships were captured – in addition, in May 1941 a U-boat, the *U-110*, was forced to surface off Iceland with a complete machine, its rotors and the key tables. This, and the extensive selection of cribs they now had, provided all the information that Hut 8 needed to break the Dolphin code from the late summer of 1941 right through to the end of the war.

Eileen Plowman arrived in the Big Room just before they started breaking the code every day. Eileen was young, only nineteen, and from Eastbourne. She'd been working for the Royal Army Service Corps records office in Hastings since she left school, which was how she came to be spotted for Bletchley.

'I had to do something to do with the war because of my age. They sent for me through the records office. I did German at school. I think that could have had a bearing on things. They told me to come for an interview to London, which I did. I didn't know London so my mother came with me. Things went from there. They wanted to know all about you. Almost why you were born. Where you were born. Everything about you.'

A few weeks later, she was sent a rail warrant and told to report to Bletchley Park.

'I had no training and I had no idea what I was going to do when I got here. I went straight into Hut 8. We were still breaking the code back then, September 1941. The code hadn't been completely broken. It was really working on breaking the German naval code. It was the professors who actually broke the codes, the real big brains. We helped them, doing what they told us to do.'

Mr Turing was living in the village pub in Shenley, the same village that Eileen was billeted in, but she barely knew him and he seemed a lot older than the girls in the Big Room who were supervised by Pat Wright and Evelyn Whatley.

'We used to get most of our instructions from Miss Whatley and Miss Wright – "Wrightie", as we used to call her. She was beautiful, very generous towards us.'

There were other more mature women in the Big Room, including the classical singer Jill Medway and Dorothy Hyson, the American actress, who had appeared in a number of popular British films. But Evelyn Whatley was the mother figure in overall charge of 'Miss Whatley's Girls'.

The impact of the ability to break the Dolphin Enigma was astonishing. Between March and June 1941, the U-boats had sunk as many as a hundred Allied ships a month. From July, the figure dropped to around forty and by November to just two, with the breaking of the Dolphin Enigma and the ability it gave the Admiralty to route the convoys around the wolf packs being the main reason. It allowed Britain's vital supplies to be replenished and kept the country going through the worst period of the war.

Despite the brilliance of people like Alan Turing, the naval Enigma could not have been broken without the Bombes. Colette St George-Yorke remembered that on one occasion while she was home on leave, she and her father went to the cinema and watched a film about the Atlantic convoys.

'I remember my father saying: "I don't understand how they knew where those U-boats were," and I had to say nothing. It was surprising how you managed to get into the habit of not saying anything about your work when you went home.'

Morag Maclennan and her friends couldn't help but feel better when they were working on 'a porpoise job' dealing with the naval Enigma for Hut 8.

'Unless you were very lucky your eight-hour watch wouldn't necessarily produce a good stop that broke a code. Sometimes you might have a good day and two of the jobs you were working on would break a code and that was a great feeling, particularly if it was a naval code. Obviously, we hoped to do it for everybody. But there was an extra little surge of pride if it was a navy one.'

Joan Clarke even went to the trouble of spending a week working alongside the Wrens on the Bombes so she could better understand how they did their job in the hope it might help her improve the way Hut 8 provided them with cribs.

Shortly before they managed to break into Dolphin on a regular basis, Joan and Alan Turing had spent the week's leave they were allowed every three months cycling and walking in North Wales. It was then that he finally decided that a relationship with a woman would never work for him, breaking the news to her on their return. They agreed it was best to break off the engagement. He came off shift work so they didn't have to see each other so often and although both were hurt by the experience, Joan's knowledge of his reasons – the only person in the hut, probably the only person at Bletchley, who knew of his homosexuality – formed a bond between them.

Joan's salary of little over £2 a week was ridiculous for someone performing the sort of work she was doing so she was promoted to linguist; this had nothing to do with her linguistic ability and was just a way of trying to get her, as a woman, more pay.

'I enjoyed answering the questionnaire with "grade – Linguist, languages – none", rather than mentioning school French and a smattering of German and Italian from reading mathematical books. My next promotion was apparently harder to negotiate, possibly because of my sex. Commander Travis stopped me in the corridor to say that they might have to put me in the WRNS to be adequately paid.'

By September 1941, there were around four hundred men and a thousand women at Bletchley, including around two hundred women with honours degrees or their Cambridge equivalents who were graded as linguists, earning anything between £104 a year to £195, while men doing comparable jobs were on the next grade up, junior assistant, earning between £300 and £400 a year.

The Treasury had agreed to increase the money paid to 'lady linguists' to between £150 and £234 but was resisting promoting all bar a very few women to junior assistant, even though that would still give them less than the men on the same grade, with female junior assistants paid around £50 a year less than their male counterparts. The Treasury was adamant.

'If it is desired to recommend any women for promotion to Junior Assistant, full particulars of their work (a) academic or other qualifications, (b) details of the work

Above: The codebreakers arriving at Bletchley Park in August 1939 in preparation for war. *Courtesy of Barbara Eachus*

Below: Miss Vacani teaching debutantes to curtsey. © *Fox Photos/Stringer/Getty Images*

left: Diana Russell-Clarke marrying Dennis Babbage in 1940. *Courtesy of Barbara Eachus*

below: A Second World War recruitment poster for the Women's Royal Naval Service, better known as the Wrens. © *IWM (PST 8286)*

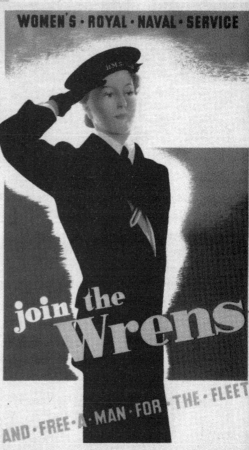

left: The Enigma machine was used by the German armed forces to encode their messages. © *Chris Howes/Wild Places Photography/Alamy*

left: The Hut 6 Decoding Room.
Crown Copyright, reproduced by permission Director GCHQ

right: The Duddery with an Enigma machine sat on the table in the foreground. *Crown Copyright, reproduced by permission Director GCHQ*

below: Two Wrens working on the Colossus computer.
Crown Copyright, reproduced by permission Director GCHQ

above: A group of codebreakers watching a game of rounders. Barbara Eachus (née Abernethy) is sat in the centre. Commander Alastair Denniston is standing on the right. *Courtesy of Barbara Eachus*

left: Jane Fawcett (née Hughes) right, with Elizabeth Blandy, who recruited Jane to Bletchley Park. *Courtesy of Jane Fawcett*

left: Sheila Lawn (née Mackenzie) who broke German naval codes in Hut 4. *Courtesy of Sheila Lawn*

right: From left to right: Sarah 'Sally' Astor (née Norton, later Baring), Diana Lyttleton (sister of the jazz musician Humphrey Lyttleton), Osla Henniker-Major (née Benning) and Jean Campbell-Harris attending a wedding. *Courtesy of Baroness Trumpington*

above: A cartoon of a number of the women who worked in Hut 4, from left to right: Fay Cooke, Françoise Knapp, Pierette Knapp, Vivian Martin, Bettaney Hansford, Adrienne Farrell, Jacqueline Simpson, Sheila Restler, Penelope Bishop, Morag Maclennan and Osla Benning. *Courtesy of the Bletchley Park Trust*

left: Pilot Warrant Officer Graham Murray, boyfriend of Colette St George-Yorke. He was shot down after dropping supplies to the resistance ahead of D-Day. *Courtesy of Colette Cook*

below: Colette Cook (née St George-Yorke). *Courtesy of Colette Cook*

below left: The JappyWaaf outside the School of Oriental and African Studies during their Japanese course. Back row from left to right: Cicely Naismith (hidden), Peggy Jackson, Margaret Brabbs and Evelyn Curtis. Front row from left to right: Denise Gifford-Hull, Eileen Barker and Mary Wisbey. *Courtesy of Mary Every*

below right: The JappyWaaf on their fiftieth anniversary weekend when they first revealed to each other what they did at Bletchley. Back row from left to right: Peggy Fletcher (née Jackson), Mary Every (née Wisbey), Margaret MacNair (née Brabbs), Eileen Barker (née Clarke). Front row from left to right: Denise Moller (née Gifford-Hull), Evelyn Sladden (née Curtis), Cicely Naismith. *Courtesy of Mary Every*

above: Alfred Dillwyn 'Dilly' Knox (standing) with, from right to left, Margaret Rock, his wife Olive and two friends.
Courtesy of Charles and Jane Foster

left: Christine Brooke-Rose.
© *Mary Evans Picture Library/IDA KAR*

right: Keith and Mavis Batey (née Lever). *Courtesy of the Batey family*

above: Troops coming ashore on the Normandy beaches on D-Day. © *TopFoto*

above: Marigold Freeman-Attwood (née Philips). *Courtesy of Marigold Freeman-Attwood*

left: Roma Davies (née Stenning). *Courtesy of Roma Davies*

on which employed and (c) a good reason why upgrading as a linguist at £234 a year is insufficient should be given.'

Despite their low pay, the linguists were paid better than most of the women at Bletchley who were graded as temporary clerks on anything from 30 shillings and six-pence (£1.52½) to 64 shillings (£3.20) a week. Inevitably the duller, more routine work was carried out by women. Most men had to serve on the front line and only those bright enough to break the codes or write the intelligence reports were allowed to work at Bletchley Park rather than be posted to fighting units, said Joan Clarke.

'At one time there was a move to increase the pay of those who had qualifications which were not relevant, which I knew about through hearing some of the girls discussing whether one of them might benefit as a trained hairdresser; but I never heard the result.'

By now the women in Hut 8 were working flat out. The hut was divided into four sections. The Registration Room, where the traffic arrived and was sorted by young women; the Banburismus Room, where the Seniors tried to cut the number of possible keys using a system of punched paper Banbury sheets; the Crib Room, where the codebreakers worked out possible cribs for use on the Bombes; and the Big Room where female clerks punched up the messages on the Banbury sheets and decoded the messages using the Typex machines modified to work like Enigma machines. The vast majority of the girls in the Big Room were like Pat Wright, in their late teens or early twenties, but whereas before Dolphin was broken there had been time to have a laugh, she and the girls were now working nonstop.

'Sometimes we had to wait a long time. Sometimes it was done quickly. But there was always a backlog of work. So we were never not doing anything.'

Nancy Harrison had been trained as a nurse immediately after leaving school in the summer of 1939 and joined the Red Cross, working in a Voluntary Aid Detachment nursing wounded soldiers at a military hospital on Salisbury Plain.

'I was no good at languages or mathematics; I loved acting and sang in the choir but I wasn't at all clever scholastically.'

But when she left the Red Cross in 1942, she was called to the Foreign Office and was made to sign the Official Secrets Act before being sent to Bletchley along with her younger sister Patricia, who was a FANY driving the shooting brakes.

'My first billet was in Bedford and I came to Bletchley by train; I was with a nice family without a bath. We all bathed in the kitchen. My father wrote to Bletchley about that! I was summoned to the billeting officer who told me off and said: "Do remember there is a war on, Miss Harrison!" Then I moved to Stony Stratford, a very nice couple who looked after me very well; I was so lucky, they were such a nice couple – and they had a bath!'

Nancy was set to work punching Banbury sheets, which were used for an ingenious system invented by Alan Turing which reduced the number of possible rotor orders that had to be tested from 336 to as little as six, making it easier for the Bombes to find a crib. The Banbury sheets, so named only because they were printed in Banbury, were about ten inches wide and several feet long. They had columns of alphabets printed vertically on them, giving horizontal lines of As, Bs, Cs, etc. Nancy punched the letters of each message into a sheet and then the Seniors in the Banburismus Room placed them over each other and matched up the punched holes to work out the possible rotor orders. Like many of the women working at Bletchley, Nancy had no idea how her work fitted into the overall picture – she just knew it was important she did what she was told to do.

'I was doing a strange job working on Banburies – enormous long sheets filled with little alphabets A to Z. I knew nothing about them and they made no sense whatsoever; I think there were comparisons, letters that had to be knocked through and compared, all the little A's and B's were gathered. I can remember running down the corridors with them in a great rush.'

For the Seniors, working in the Banburismus Room was highly enjoyable, like working out a complex puzzle, with the added reward that if you solved it you were well on the way to breaking the code. Joan found it 'enthralling' and since she cycled to and from work and didn't have to wait for transport she would frequently stay on well beyond her shift to solve a Banbury puzzle.

But on 1 February 1942 it all came to a halt. The U-boats introduced a new Enigma machine which had four rotors instead of three. Hut 8 had no chance of breaking the new system, codenamed Shark. The vital intelligence the Admiralty was using to re-route the Atlantic convoys around the wolf packs disappeared. Alan Turing was working on other things so Hugh Alexander took over as head of

Hut 8. Hugh Alexander was one of the leading code-breakers at Bletchley, but even he couldn't break Shark.

Fortunately for Britain, during the first half of 1942 the U-boats concentrated on attacking US ships off the US coastline, but in August they resumed their attacks on the Atlantic convoys with eighty-six U-boats – four times as many as they'd had before – sinking eleven Allied ships in a single attack.

Over the next two months the U-boats located a third of the Allied supply convoys, sinking forty-three ships, and in November, with the number of supply ships sunk close to the hundred mark for that month alone, the Admiralty came close to accusing Hut 8 not only of not doing its job but of not understanding that this wasn't about solving interesting puzzles. If Bletchley didn't break the Shark Enigma, Britain could lose the Battle of the Atlantic and the vital supply lines from America.

The tensions were understandable but the criticism was unfair. Everyone from Hugh Alexander right down to the girls in the Big Room was working as hard as they could to break the code. No one in Hut 8 was under any illusion that thousands of sailors' lives and quite possibly Britain's ability to keep the war going was under threat. The 'Shark Blackout', as it was known at Bletchley, was to be one of the most depressing times for anyone at the Park. Pat Wright remembered it as a terrible time.

'The Atlantic convoys coming across were being sunk and we were told that if they could just keep decoding these messages then they would keep the submarines away from the convoys.'

She and the even younger girls like Eileen Plowman felt their responsibility very heavily. They didn't need to be told that lives were being lost; many of them had boyfriends or brothers who were putting their own lives at risk. Eileen was in no doubt about how important it was that everyone in Hut 8 worked as hard as they possibly could.

'We used to find it very nerve-racking. We used to get uptight about it all. The responsibility of it. I wasn't very old. I think at that time I was very King and country. It was something that was important.'

But despite the frustrations in the Admiralty and Hut 8, the solution was already in hand. At the end of October 1942 the crew of the *U-559* scuttled the submarine in the Mediterranean after being attacked by the British destroyer HMS *Petard*. The *Petard*'s first officer, Lieutenant Anthony Fasson, and Able-Seaman Colin Grazier swam to the U-boat and passed the codebooks out to sixteen-year-old Naafi boy Tommy Brown, but before the seamen could get out the *U-559* sank, taking them down with it. They were awarded the George Cross posthumously. Brown received the George Medal. Their heroism was vital in helping to end the blackout.

The codebooks were for lower-grade German naval codes but the messages they were used to encode were also sent to other ships that only used the Shark code. If they could track identical messages they should have a crib that would get them back into the U-boat codes.

Shaun Wylie took over the codebreaking shift in Hut 8 at midnight on 12 December 1942. They worked through the night trying to match the messages broken with the codebooks against Enigma messages without luck. Next morning, a frustrated Shaun Wylie was having breakfast in the new canteen that had replaced the restaurant in the mansion when someone from Hut 8 rushed in and grabbed him excitedly:

'We're back into the U-boats.'

Shaun Wylie was elated and relieved. In a measure of how important it was not just to Bletchley and the Admiralty but also to the country itself, he was under orders to ring Commander Travis, who had taken over from Commander Denniston as the head of Bletchley Park, immediately the code was broken, day or night. Commander Travis had exactly the same instructions from his own boss, Stewart Menzies, the head of MI6, and Menzies had been left in no uncertain terms that he was to inform Mr Churchill immediately.

The girls in the Big Room were soon dealing with a flood of messages to decode as the codebreakers began cracking first the day's code and then the settings for previous days. Huge numbers of messages had piled up and it was important to track the latest position for each of the different U-boats. Eileen Plowman remembered the messages coming through thick and fast.

'It got more intense once it was broken. They used to say they were breaking "the day". We would set the machines up and then all the messages – there were lots and lots of messages – came through and everybody went mad with all the decoding and it all came out in German. Where I came in useful was that I knew German, because it was all positions of the U-boats and we had to get that right and send up to Admiralty. The next thing you'd hear was that a U-boat had been sunk.'

Within hours, the Admiralty was once more routing the Atlantic convoys around the wolf packs and from then on Hut 8 had no problems breaking the U-boat codes.

Once the code had been broken and Pat and the other girls in the Big Room had typed out the strips of German and stuck them on the back of the original messages, they were passed through to Phoebe in Hut 4 and handed on to the naval intelligence reporters. The Z Watch, which wrote the intelligence reports on all the German naval Enigma messages, was run by Walter Ettinghausen, a German Jew who had fled the Nazis with his family and become an Oxford academic. He joined the British Army in September 1940, but since he was one of the leading German scholars in the country it was not long before he was sent to Bletchley.

The reports would come into the Z Watch in batches in wire trays and the distribution of the messages was controlled by two Wrens. One of them, Diana Spence, was twenty-two when she arrived at Bletchley. She was astonished to find that her billet was the 'majestic' Woburn Abbey and her 'cabin' was in a room that had once been the Duke of Bedford's private bedchamber; it was covered with beautifully ornate and obviously antique Chinese wallpaper. Diana and the other Wren sat at a small table in the Z Watch waiting for batches of messages decoded by the girls in the Big Room to come in.

'We gave them out to members of the Watch, who were all interpreters, on the big table. When they'd translated the German we sent the handwritten messages back down to the typing room. The important part of our work was to check the messages when they were sent back again typed in English against the handwritten translations, in case there were any mistakes.'

The teleprinter operators typing out the reports were WAAFs rather than Wrens, but it was Diana and her fellow Wrens who controlled the messages and made sure that the often untidy handwriting of the intelligence reporters was typed out properly by the WAAFs before it was sent to the Admiralty. Unlike the women in Hut 8, they were reading reports in English and could understand what was going on. So the nine Wrens who worked in the Z Watch were in a very privileged and unusual position for women working at Bletchley in that they could see the war from very close up.

'We were always reading messages sent by U-boat commanders saying they had sighted a convoy and were about to attack. The air force would be alerted and then very often we would read a message from the same U-boat commander saying he couldn't surface to attack as the RAF were overhead. If we did not spot a mistake by a typist – in perhaps a degree of longitude or latitude – it could be vital.'

There was good communication between the reporters in the Z Watch and Hut 8 to ensure that Pat and the other girls in the Big Room didn't waste time typing out messages that were irrelevant or had no intelligence value.

'We would say, "Shall we go on with this?" And they would say: "Yes, keep going," or "No, don't bother."'

So many teenage girls had now been called up by the Foreign Office to go to Bletchley that a number of mothers were becoming concerned at what might be happening to their daughters. Peter Loxley, the senior Foreign Office official dealing with MI6 and the rest of the secret world of intelligence, wrote to Alan Bradshaw, the head administrator at Bletchley, explaining that one anxious mother had written to the head of the Foreign Office:

'She said that she and a number of other mothers were worried about the lack of supervision exercised over the many young girls who are now working at Bletchley. There seemed to be nobody who had general charge of their welfare, and she had heard several accounts of girls who were cracking under the strain.'

Commander Travis set up a Women's Committee in the spring of 1942 to look after the well-being of all women working at Bletchley, but he made it clear that 'it will not deal with questions concerning work or pay'. The committee included representatives of all the main departments and the women's services, as well as the MI6 section that encoded secret messages to its agents abroad, which was still based at Bletchley. Their representative was the very glamorous Lady Cynthia Tothill, who was well known as the 'face' of Pond's beauty creams in all of its advertisements.

The committee – whose members included Evelyn Whatley, representing all the women in Hut 8 – dealt with a number of problems ranging from the deteriorating standard of coffee served in the canteen to the theft of watches and the 'ever-increasing amount of artistry' in the ladies' cloakrooms and toilets; the problem that almost certainly most concerned the anxious mothers was presumably left to the representatives of the various sections on the committee to deal with privately.

Christmas 1943 was notable for a major triumph within Hut 8, the tracking of the *Scharnhorst*. This was the German battlecruiser that had sunk the Royal Navy's aircraft carrier HMS *Glorious* with the loss of 1,500 men in 1940 after the Admiralty ignored Harry Hinsley's warnings.

During the days leading up to Christmas, Hut 8 was on full alert with numerous indications in the messages encoded in the naval Enigma code that the *Scharnhorst* was about to attack a Royal Navy Arctic convoy taking supplies to the Russians, and that she was backed up by a number of other German warships and a wolf pack of eight U-boats. Christmas Day brought confirmation from the U-boats that they had found the convoy. What the Germans didn't know was that they were heading into a British trap. Admiral Sir Bruce Fraser, commander of the Home Fleet, who had himself captained *Glorious*, was deliberately trying to draw out the *Scharnhorst*. But it might all go worryingly wrong, and things were tense in Hut 8 as they worked hard to produce the latest intelligence for Admiral Fraser. Pat Wright had been working the day shift, typing out the messages from the U-boats reporting their sightings of the convoy.

'I finished work at four o'clock and went back to my billet. Christmas dinner was over by now but Mrs Tomlin said, "Hello, duck, saved you a bit of Christmas pudding.

Here you are. This'll make your shit black." I didn't know whether to laugh or what to do. So I said thank you very much and ate it.'

It was a touch of humour amid the worries over the convoy. Next day Pat was back in the office on the day shift as Admiral Fraser's trap was sprung in the Barents Sea north of Norway. From shortly after nine o'clock in the morning of Boxing Day 1943, the *Scharnhorst* was repeatedly attacked by Royal Navy ships and was finally sunk just before seven in the evening.

Admiral Fraser came to Bletchley to thank the code-breakers and to explain how vital their work had been. There was a ballot to hear him talk and a number of the girls in the Big Room won tickets, sitting and listening to the results of their work with a mixture of awe and pride.

By now the Americans, with more financial and manu-facturing resources, had built many more Bombes than Bletchley could afford and had taken over the bulk of the work protecting the Atlantic convoys. But Hut 8 remained busy. The Allies were about to invade France. There was a great deal of concern over the damage that the U-boats could do to the Allied invasion force as it crossed the Channel, and a special team of Wren intercept operators were brought to Bletchley to provide Hut 8 with the messages as quickly as possible.

It was clear from the restrictions on travel that D-Day was coming but Pat and the other girls didn't know when until the evening of 4 June 1944 when they went into work and were told the invasion would be launched overnight.

'They told us they wanted every message decoded as fast

as possible. But then it was postponed because the weather was so bad and that meant we girls knew it was going to take place, so we had to stay there until D-Day (for security reasons). We slept where we could, and worked when we could, and of course then they set off on 6 June, and that was D-Day.

'The next day I went back to my billet and Mrs Tomlin said, "Where the bleedin' hell have you been? We've invaded France, don't you know!" I said I'd been working so I hadn't heard the news.'

7

Dilly's Girls

Dilly Knox was deeply unhappy when the Enigma codes were taken away from him at the start of 1940. The new boy Gordon Welchman had set up Hut 6 to break the German army and air force Enigma codes and Alan Turing and Peter Twinn had gone off to work on the German naval Enigma, leaving Dilly with nothing to do. He'd been at the heart of British codebreaking successes since the start of the Great War, when he'd pieced together and decoded the charred fragments of messages from a giant German Zeppelin airship destroyed by the Russians. Without codes to break, Dilly was like a fish out of water.

When it came to piecing together fragments of secret codes, Dilly was a genius. He'd proved that when deciphering the British Museum's Greek papyrus found in an Egyptian cave and with his greatest First World War triumph, breaking the German diplomatic codes, unlocking the 1917 telegram from the German Foreign Secretary Arthur Zimmerman to the Mexicans that offered them parts of the United States if they'd join the war on Germany's side. Breaking that code was one of the most important intelligence coups of the Great War, bringing the Americans into the conflict and ensuring the Allied victory.

Dilly had broken the Italian and Spanish Enigma codes before the war and he was the only British codebreaker who'd truly believed the German Enigma codes could be broken. Finally, with a bit of help from the Poles, he'd done it. He'd have preferred to have managed it on his own, of course, but his methods – and his confidence – had been proven correct. They'd even made him chief assistant on the back of his success. In theory he was the head codebreaker, and yet he now found himself cast aside, his work on Enigma taken from him by the new boys. The Cottage Enigma codebreaking section had been closed down, his staff hived off to Hut 6 or the Naval Section, and he was hidden away on his own in a tiny office in the Park's old plum shed.

Inevitably, a resignation letter followed, complaining at the way in which the Enigma codes had been 'stolen' away from him. Just as inevitably, Commander Denniston refused to accept Dilly's resignation, rightly telling him that he had unique qualities vital for the war effort. He should put his talents to work breaking new codes and leave Hut 6 to do the day-to-day grind.

The son of a bishop, Dilly was in his mid-fifties and so wildly eccentric as to put his fellow codebreakers in the shade. He wore horn-rimmed glasses without which he could see nothing and frequently stuffed them into his tobacco pouch rather than his spectacles case by mistake. Dilly was tall, thin and bald. His trousers and jackets were too short, as if he had bought them some years earlier and outgrown them by several inches, and his face always looked drawn, as if he hadn't eaten in days.

Dilly was so absent-minded that he forgot to invite two of his three brothers to his own wedding in 1920. He had so many of his best ideas while relaxing in the bath that during the First World War he had a bathtub installed in his office in the Admiralty. At one point, his fellow codebreakers became concerned and, thinking something must have happened to him, broke into his office, only to find him sat in the bath with the plug pulled out and both taps full on while he stared at the wall deep in thought, trying to solve a coding puzzle.

Commander Denniston reopened the Cottage and put Dilly in charge of a research section looking into unbroken machine codes that Hut 6 didn't have time to deal with. Manning the section would be a problem. Although Dilly had liked and trusted Alan Turing, Peter Twinn and Tony Kendrick, he clearly had little patience with the new young men who were coming in with their own ideas of how the work should be done. They all seemed to want to make their names, to prove themselves. Dilly was naturally a loner. He was certainly not prepared to work with anyone arrogant enough to believe they could teach him how to do his job. So Denniston agreed to recruit a team of young women to help Dilly. They would swiftly become known as 'Dilly's Girls'.

The first recruits were the daughters of two members of Denniston's golf club, Joyce Fox-Male and Claire Harding, who at twenty-seven was to be office manager. As well as clerical support, Dilly needed someone to manage his codebreaking work and Denniston was keen it should be a mathematician. Margaret Rock was ideal. She was thirty-six, so just a bit older than the other girls, and had studied at Bedford College, London, before becoming a statistician. She had precisely the sort of ordered mind that Dilly needed to complement his madcap ideas, and arrived in the Cottage in April 1940.

Dilly had very clear ideas of what girls he needed in his research section. A mathematician was one of the most obvious requirements, and another was at least one German linguist, if not more. He certainly didn't want any debs whose daddies had persuaded a friend at the Foreign Office to find them a place at Bletchley. He wanted women with ability whatever their background.

Mavis Lever was already working for the Code and Cypher School when the Cottage was reopened but she was not based at Bletchley Park. Mavis was breaking commercial codes at the pre-war headquarters in Broadway Buildings in London. She'd been born in May 1921 in Dulwich, south London; her father worked in the local postal sorting office and her mother was a seamstress. Mavis attended Coloma Convent School in West Croydon where she studied German as one of her languages. As a child she and her parents traditionally took their holidays in Bournemouth but in the 1930s Joseph Goebbels, Hitler's propaganda chief, had created a programme of cheap holidays to Germany under the title of *Kraft durch Freude* ('Strength through Joy') and in 1936 at the age of fifteen Mavis persuaded her mother and father that this year they should go to the Rhineland.

'We bought cheap tickets for a steamer trip along the River Rhine. We joined crowds of happy German workers with free tickets. They were to be indoctrinated into the myths and legends of German heroes. Wagner's blonde Rhine Maidens were with us constantly and the band struck up as we passed the Lorelei. I lapped it all up and when I got back decided to opt for German literature in the sixth form.'

Mavis earned a place at University College London studying German Romanticism under Professor Leonard Willoughby, one of Dilly's closest colleagues in Room 40 during the First World War. Mavis was due to go to Tübingen University in Germany for a term in 1938 but, with war increasingly likely, she was switched to Zurich University instead.

'I stayed there until war was imminent and by the time I got home the Siegfried Line between France and Germany was being manned so I just got back to UCL in time and found they were evacuating to Aberystwyth. I wanted to do something better for the war effort than read poetry in Wales, so I said I'd train as a nurse, but I was told: "Oh, no you don't. Not with your German."'

Mavis was interviewed at the Foreign Office and selected as an ideal candidate for a job in intelligence but her suitability for secret work was put briefly under the spotlight after two German 'Jewish' refugees she had sponsored at UCL, helping them to find work at a country house in Kent, were arrested as spies. Eventually she was cleared of anything but naivety and sent to the MI6 headquarters at 54 Broadway, opposite St James's underground station.

'I was getting rather excited. I thought I might be going to be a spy, Mata Hari, seducing Prussian officers. But I don't think either my legs or my German were good enough because they sent me to the Government Code and Cypher School.'

She sat in London examining commercial codes and perusing the personal columns of *The Times* for coded spy messages, but in May 1940, after showing promise with a piece of smart lateral thinking that uncovered the origin of an illegal shipment to Germany, Mavis was plucked out and sent to Bletchley to be the German linguist in Dilly's new research team. His welcome was typical of the way he threw new recruits in at the deep end and Mavis's response immediately endeared her to him.

'I reported to Commander Denniston and Barbara Abernethy, his secretary, took me over to see Dilly. He was sat by the window wreathed in smoke. He said: "Hello. Have you got a pencil? We're breaking machines." I hadn't a clue what he meant. He handed me a pile of utter gibberish and said: "Here, have a go." It was covered in his purple inky scrawls. "But I'm afraid it's all Greek to me," I said. Dilly burst into delighted laughter and said: "I wish it were." I was very embarrassed later to discover that he was a distinguished Greek scholar.'

There was more to Dilly's choices than excluding any hint of masculine competitiveness from the research section. All the girls were carefully chosen for their capabilities. Commander Denniston had picked Claire Harding for her administrative ability. Margaret Rock, the mathematician, and Mavis Lever, one of several German linguists, were joined by speech therapist Joyce Mitchell, and three actresses, all of whom were selected by Dilly because their training would give them an understanding of the rhythms of the messages. Mavis was adamant that it was nothing to do with Dilly wanting to be surrounded by pretty young women. He was no womaniser.

'He put women on pedestals. He was a great admirer of Lewis Carroll and for me Dilly was Alice's White Knight, endearingly eccentric and always so concerned about one's welfare. The girls he chose had a background connected with linguistics or phonetics or literature. It was all a question of linguistic patterns of syllables for him. Others provided by Commander Denniston had secretarial training and acted as registrars.'

Dilly had a unique knack of using his imagination to open up codes.

'He would stuff his pipe with sandwiches instead of tobacco he was so woolly-minded. But he was brilliant, absolutely brilliant. It just seemed to come naturally to him. He said the most extraordinary things. "Which way does the clock go round?" And if you were stupid enough to say clockwise, he'd just say: "Oh no it doesn't, not if you're the clock, it's the opposite way." And that's sometimes how you had to think about the machines. Not just to look at them how you saw them but what was going on inside.'

Dilly's unusual views on training left new recruits to sink or swim but ensured that Mavis, along with Margaret and the other girls, developed their ability to think laterally. Very often, Dilly would sleep in the Cottage, working late into the night, surviving on black coffee and chocolate and only returning to his home at Courns Wood, thirty miles south of Bletchley, at the weekend. While the young girls were frustrated by Dilly's inability to explain things simply, they clearly adored him, none more so than Mavis.

'It was a strange little outfit in the Cottage. Organisation is not a word you would associate with Dilly Knox. I remember the amount of time we spent searching for his specs and tobacco tin hidden under stacks of Enigma messages and how when preoccupied he mistook the cupboard for the door.'

The month after Mavis arrived, Italy entered the war and she was put to work on the Italian Navy's Enigma code.

'I had hardly begun to make head or tail of the Enigma codes and was doing the most menial tasks before Italy came into the war and I was put on to Italian, with only the scantiest knowledge of the language and the tiniest pocket Italian dictionary to work with. So it was quite a challenge.'

Dilly was keen to find out if the machine the Italians were using was the same one that he'd broken in 1938, but because the Italian Navy was now dealing with naval movements across the Mediterranean rather than just the Spanish Civil War, the messages were completely different and none of the 'cribs', the original text that Dilly had used before to break the code, were of any use.

When he was breaking the Spanish and Italian Enigma machines in the 1930s, Dilly had devised a system of rods, strips of cardboard with a row of letters in the order they appeared in the wiring of each Enigma rotor which were slid along under the encoded text to try to find a point at which the text of the crib began to appear. It turned the complex task of codebreaking into a word puzzle like a crossword, which Mavis found particularly easy.

'Many of the girls never understood how the machine worked but they were excellent at rodding. We called it a game. It was like a game of Scrabble or like doing a crossword. But it did require a lot of patience as there were seventy-eight positions to try out for the three rotors. You would have to work at it very, very hard and it made you pink-eyed. After you'd done it for a few hours you wondered whether you'd ever see anything when it was before your eyes.'

The lack of cribs was a problem but when Dilly first broke the Italian Enigma all of the messages began with the Italian word *per* [for], to indicate who the message was for, so he told the girls to look for a rodding sequence that would produce PER, plus an X, which was used to indicate a space between words. For three months, they tried to break the code without success. No one could get PERX to fit. Then in September 1940, Mavis made the crucial breakthrough.

'I was all on my own one night and I couldn't put up PERX. It put up PER but not an X. It kept putting up an S. I thought, supposing it's not PERX, it might be PERSONALE then PER as in "personal for . . ." so I put up the rods for PERSONALE and then I got X and then PERX and then it went off beautifully all down the line.'

After a couple of spaces, she found there was a 'GN', which was the middle of SIGNOR, so she knew the two missing spaces were SI and the three spaces afterwards were OR and then X.

'So I filled in my beautiful Italian crossword puzzle and when Dilly came in the next morning, I had the whole text of the message. He couldn't believe it. Well, I couldn't believe it either because it was so easy, but it was simply because I was following Dilly's methods.'

Dilly was impressed. He went to Commander Denniston and insisted Mavis must have a wage rise from 35 shillings (£1.75) a week, the rate for a temporary clerk, to the proper rate for a linguist of 57 shillings and sixpence (£2.88). He also promoted her from the backroom to work with him in 'the front room' as one of his assistants along with Margaret Rock.

'He took me out to dinner at the Fountain Inn on the Stony Stratford road to celebrate. It was my first experience of being driven in Dilly's Baby Austin. Being driven anywhere by Dilly was a nightmare, especially in the blackout. There were tank traps down Watling Street and he just drove straight through them. They were slightly shaken.'

Mavis was lucky with her billet. She was sent to a farm at Leighton Buzzard where the farmer's wife immediately understood that the work Mavis and the other young women billeted with her were doing was secret and she mustn't ask any questions. She also seemed to realise that their work was important and appreciated the way that Mavis helped on the farm.

'She would insist on bringing us a cup of tea in the morning. She suddenly said: "I shan't be here next week. My aunt will be looking after you. I'm having a baby, you know." And we felt so awful that we'd let her wait on us. We had no idea and she laughed and just said: "You're not the only ones who can keep a secret, you know."'

Working as one of Dilly's assistants was very demanding, but also exhilarating. Mavis and Margaret had trouble keeping track of all the brilliant ideas he had to find ways into the codes.

'Dilly's ideas just went off like a Catherine Wheel. He just had bright idea after bright idea. Margaret Rock would be trying to work out what he said yesterday and I'd be trying to pin down something he said today and there were so many of these things that perhaps we had six bright ideas to work through and one of them would work. It was a strange form of lateral thinking that brings in a lot of memory. But if he hadn't had us to pin those bright ideas down for him I think perhaps it wouldn't have worked so well.'

The problem with Dilly's rods was that eventually the Italians would change the wiring of the rotors and the rods would be no use – they would no longer match the new configuration. Then they would have to find out the wiring and create new rods, a complex task. The dreaded moment when they were no longer able to decode the messages came in November 1940. Fortunately, in order to maintain a steady stream of messages so the Allies didn't know that the sudden appearance of a long message meant something was about to happen, the Italians sent out a number of fake messages, which Dilly called 'duds'.

Mavis was working the night shift when she noticed there was something wrong with a message. They were so used to looking for unusual things in messages that she spotted immediately why it looked odd.

'I picked up this message and thought: there's not a single L in this.'

The main flaw of the Enigma machine, seen by the inventors as a security-enhancing measure, was that it would never encode a letter as itself. But the operator of this particular message had turned the security aspect on its head by tearing up the rule book and letting the codebreakers in.

'My chap had been told to send out a dummy message and he'd just had a fag and pressed the last key of the middle row of his keyboard, the L. So that was the only letter that didn't come out.'

Mavis now had the longest crib anyone could have had. Because there was no L in the received text she knew that the original message must have been just a string of L's, so she should be able to work out the wiring of the new wheel. But the fact that it was all the same letter added some complications and Mavis wasn't sure how to get over them.

'So I went over to Hut 6 and found one of the mathematicians there and he very kindly volunteered to help me.'

Mavis and the Hut 6 mathematician, Keith Batey, sat in the Cottage drinking chicory coffee and trying to work out the wiring together, in contravention of Civil Service regulations preventing men and women working together on night shifts in such small numbers. Mavis thought Keith was rather nice and decided to test him out, dropping her pencil to see how he would react, hoping that he would gallantly bend down to pick it up for her. It didn't work. Keith looked down at the pencil, looked at Mavis and said, 'You've dropped your pencil,' leaving Mavis to pick it back up and continue working out the wiring of the new rotor.

'Together with lots of coffee and a much more logical approach we did in fact break the wiring. I'd like to say it was love at first sight because he was my husband-to-be. But it wasn't unfortunately.' Despite Keith's lack of gallantry over the pencil – he realised what Mavis was doing and decided not to play ball – they did eventually begin courting, although not until a year later when he was seconded to work in the Cottage. 'But we liked to remember that our life together began with an L dud.'

Next morning, Dilly saw his trust in Mavis vindicated with another triumph in uncovering the wiring of the new rotor. The fact that they could keep on top of the Italian Navy's Enigma machine, thanks to Mavis and a bit of assistance from Keith, was to bring the Royal Navy one of its greatest victories of the Second World War. In late March 1941, Mavis decoded a message which said simply: 'Today's the day minus three.'

'So of course we knew the Italian Navy was going to do something in three days' time. Why they had to say that I can't imagine. It seems rather daft, but they did. So we worked for three days. It was all the nail-biting stuff of keeping up all night working.'

Dilly's Girls didn't go home, they sat in the Cottage, pouncing on the motorcycle dispatch riders bringing the intercepted messages from the RAF wireless station at Chicksands then busily sliding the rods under the messages and filling in the letters to find out precisely what the Italian Navy was planning to do. They became very bleary-eyed, sometimes wondering if it wouldn't be better to go home and get some sleep and then start again in the morning.

'Then a very, very long message came in which was practically the battle orders. How many cruisers there were, and how many submarines were to be there, and where they were to be at such and such a time; absolutely incredible that they should spell it all out.'

The Italian intention was to intercept British convoys en route from Egypt to Greece. It was pouring with rain when they finished the translation and Mavis rushed it across to be teleprinted to Admiral Sir Andrew Cunningham, the Commander-in-Chief of the Mediterranean Fleet, at his headquarters in Alexandria, Egypt. The battle plan was so detailed and so audacious that at first he didn't believe it, Mavis said. But John Godfrey, an old friend of Dilly's, told the admiral he could trust Dilly and his girls to get it right.

'The marvellous thing about Admiral Cunningham was that he played it extremely cool. He knew that they were going to go out and confront the Italian fleet at Matapan but he did a real Drake on them.'

The Japanese were not yet in the war so there was still a Japanese consul in Alexandria. But the Japanese were already allied to the Germans and the Italians, so their consul was spying on the British. The consul was a keen golfer, so Admiral Cunningham ostentatiously went to the golf course with his clubs and his overnight bag and checked in, knowing that the consul would see him and report it.

'He pretended he was just going to have the weekend off and made sure the Japanese spy would pass it all back. Then, under cover of the night, he took the Mediterranean Fleet out and confronted the Italians.'

The Italians were caught completely by surprise and the Royal Navy ships sank three Italian heavy cruisers and two destroyers with the loss of 3,000 Italian sailors. The Italian Navy would never attempt to take on its British counterparts again.

'It was very exciting stuff. A message came through from Admiral Godfrey at midnight. "Tell Dilly, we have won a great victory in the Mediterranean and it's all thanks to him and his girls." Well, imagine what that was like to a bunch of nineteen-year-olds. We were jubilant.'

They'd been working for three days with no time off, taking breaks for food in the mansion dining room when they could and sleeping for brief periods on the floor of the Cottage while they waited for the dispatch riders to bring in more messages from Chicksands. Finally, it was over.

'After three nights we were free and I was hoping to get a train, and of course it was much too late, but when I got to Bletchley station the *Royal Scot* was taking on water. So I went up to the engine driver and said, "Do you think you could give me a lift to Leighton Buzzard?" and he said, "I'd do anything for you, missie, but this train won't go into Leighton Buzzard." So I went to sleep on the station until the milk train came through.'

Over the next week, the news about what was dubbed the Battle of Matapan began to leak out into the papers and eventually to Pathé News, the cinema newsreel that was the main way that people living in Britain got to see what was actually happening in the war. Mavis and the rest of Dilly's Girls were thrilled to see the battle going on because it helped them to understand how much of an impact they could have on the war.

'It was on all the cinema screens and we would have loved to tell our parents we had a hand in it, but we couldn't, of course.'

A month or so later, Admiral Cunningham came to Bletchley to thank Dilly and his girls for what they'd done. Mavis and a few of the other girls rushed down to the Eight Bells pub at the end of the road from the Park to buy some bottles of wine.

'We all thought him very handsome and dashing, especially when he drank a toast to Dilly and his girls for virtually having put the Italian Navy out of action for the rest of the war.'

They might have played a large part in a famous victory but they were still mostly teenage girls, laughing and giggling at the distinguished admiral and itching to play a joke on him. Unfortunately for Admiral Cunningham, the walls of the Cottage had just been whitewashed.

'We thought it would be jolly funny if we could talk to him and get him to lean against the wet whitewash in his lovely dark-blue uniform and then go away with a white stern. So that's what we did. It's rather terrible, isn't it? On the one hand, everything's so organised to try to win the

war and on the other these silly young things are trying
to snare the admiral. We tried not to giggle when he left.'

The Matapan success led to greatly reduced Italian
Navy activity, which was reflected in the smaller number
of messages being sent. The job of dealing with these
was passed to the Naval Section and Dilly and his girls
began work on what was to be their greatest triumph. MI5
had captured most of the German spies sent to Britain
and turned them back as 'double agents', feeding the
Germans false information designed to deceive them in
an operation known as the Double Cross system.

It was run by the Double Cross Committee, a team of
British intelligence officers who controlled the information
that was sent back to the German secret service, the Abwehr.
They also controlled the agents' wireless links – MI5
wireless operators sent the actual messages – so they had
all the relatively simple codes the double agents had been
given. Other agents across Europe used similar codes and
wireless links so it was fairly easy for Bletchley Park to break
them all. But the main links between the Abwehr officers
running the German agents and their bosses in Hamburg
and Berlin used a highly complex Enigma machine to
encode their messages and Hut 6 couldn't break it. The
Double Cross Committee could use the double agents to
feed false intelligence to the Germans but they had no
idea whether or not it was believed in Berlin.

Hut 6 couldn't break the Abwehr Enigma so they gave
it to Dilly. This would keep him occupied, keep him
quiet, just as the Italian Enigma machine had done. The
Abwehr Enigma had four rotors instead of the standard

three and, unlike other machines, they turned over much more frequently with no easily predictable pattern so that a number of rotors, occasionally all four, turned over at the same time. The Germans believed this made it impossible to break and at Bletchley, especially among Mr Welchman's mathematicians, there were doubts that even Dilly could crack it.

This was to be Dilly's last big codebreaking challenge. He'd been diagnosed with lymphatic cancer shortly before the war and in the summer of 1941 the doctors found a secondary cancer. Nothing was going to beat Dilly this time round, not the cancer and especially not the Abwehr Enigma. He called it the 'Spy Enigma' and in a moment of inspiration while working on his own in the Cottage he realised that, just like Mavis's Italian Enigma success, the feature the German spies believed made the code most secure – in this case the frequent turnover of all four rotors at the same time – was precisely the point where it was most vulnerable. Mavis remembered the breakthrough.

'We always made sure that one of Dilly's Girls would be on duty in the Cottage for him and it was a new girl, Phyllida Cross, who was on that evening when he rushed through to the backroom in excitement and tried to explain his brain wave. She couldn't understand a word and all she could do was to make more black coffee for him and try to put his papers in order, which was always a hopeless task.'

Dilly was fond of using odd names for things, rather like Lewis Carroll, and he called the moments when all four rotors turned over at the same time either 'crabs' or 'lobsters'. The four-rotor turnovers often came close together in pairs. Dilly called these pairs of turnovers crabs and dismissed them as no use at all to the codebreakers. He realised they needed to find what he called the lobsters, the four-rotor turnovers which were on their own not in pairs. They were likely to be followed by a much longer stream of text without any rotors turning over at all. This was the point where 'the Spy Enigma' would be vulnerable to attack.

Next morning he was waiting for Mavis and Margaret at the door, overcome with excitement, and said: 'If two cows are crossing the road, there must be a point where there is only one and that's what we must find.' The cow on its own was the lobster. If they could track down the lobster, they could get into the code. Dilly's theory of crabs, lobsters and cows was 'Alice in Wonderland' logic and incomprehensible to most people but Mavis and Margaret understood what he was talking about. Dilly instigated a 'lobster hunt' and after two days Mavis found 'a perfect lobster' which allowed him to work out the turnover patterns of one of the wheels.

Mavis and Margaret now began systematically looking for messages where his ideas would work, with Mavis trawling through the Enigma messages between Berlin and German intelligence officers in the Balkans and Margaret looking at the messages between Germany and Spain. But with the cancer having an increasing impact, Mavis could see her boss was completely drained.

'Dilly collapsed when he went home after weeks of working day and night with little to eat and battling with cancer. Thereafter he only made fleeting visits when brought over by his wife Olive.'

Margaret went to Courns Wood to work alongside Dilly while Mavis took charge of the Cottage, aged just twenty and on the basic £150-a-year salary of a female linguist. On 8 December 1941 she broke into a message on the link between Belgrade and Berlin, allowing the reconstruction of one of the rotors. Mavis was elated by her success, which proved that the Italian naval Enigma breaks hadn't simply been lucky – although she would say that luck was always the key.

'Dilly and I were never worried about probability; it was serendipity that counted and it seemed to me that there was a good chance of finding lobsters and sometimes it worked and sometimes it didn't, and this time it did.'

Commander Denniston wrote to Stewart Menzies, the head of MI6, to let him know of the success: 'Knox has again justified his reputation as our most original investigator of Enigma problems. He read one message on December 8th. He attributes the success to two young girl members of his staff Miss Rock and Miss Lever, and he gives them all the credit. He is of course the leader, but no doubt has selected and trained his staff to assist him in his somewhat unusual methods.'

From that point on, Bletchley was reading all the high-level messages between the German intelligence officers running the double agents and Berlin, and the Double Cross Committee knew with absolute certainty that the Germans believed all of the false intelligence they were being fed.

Two months later, Mavis broke a second Abwehr machine, the GGG, which was used between the German intelligence officers in Spain, where most of the agent runners were based. Little wonder that when questioned by the Hut 6 mathematicians over his use of 'Dilly's Girls' and how effective they were, Dilly invoked one of the most famous discoveries of the ancient Greek mathematician Archimedes:

'Give me a Rock and a Lever and I can move the universe.'

The new material was codenamed ISK, standing for Illicit Signals Knox, and a new section was set up to decode it. Dilly might have been largely housebound by the cancer, but it didn't stop him looking for the additional girls he needed to work in his new ISK Section.

Jean Orme lived in Wendover, ten miles north of Dilly's home at Courns Wood and on his route into Bletchley Park, so when her name was put forward by one of his other girls, he stopped off to interview her himself. Jean's father was the village doctor.

'I didn't get off to the best of starts because I had a terrible cold so I was still in bed when he arrived. It must have been quite early. He asked me if I knew any German. He said it might be useful to know a few words. He was clearly not a well man. He spent most of the time telling me about the people who worked in the Cottage, including one woman who he said was really nice but who wore trousers and a bow tie, and smoked a pipe.'

At any event, after going back to school to learn some basic German, Jean was put to work in the ISK Section. She hadn't done brilliantly on her School Certificate and didn't expect to go to university, so it was something of a surprise to her that Dilly thought her suitable for the work.

'I was seventeen. I was shy and a bit naive. I had tried to join the Wrens but I wasn't actually old enough. I suppose someone must have shown me what to do. It was a bit like a crossword puzzle. One became quite good at it. I found it was something I could do. There was an awful lot of luck and chance, but I enjoyed doing it, that's half the battle.'

Jean's mother, who was a senior member of the British Legion, used her contacts to arrange a safe billet for her daughter with a Baptist minister and his wife in Stony Stratford, even though Jean's family were all devout Roman Catholics.

'They were very kind. I think it must have been a thankless task: they were paid twenty-one shillings a week and we worked strange hours. After about eighteen months, I got more independent and decided to move into the women's hostel just outside the gate initially, but I could only stay there for about six months. I was then given a billet in Buckingham with a young woman whose husband was in the army in Italy. She had a seven-year-old daughter. She was very kind.'

In her spare time, Jean played tennis on the courts beside the Cottage, went to the beer hut with her friends and to the dances held once a month in the main assembly hall; this was just outside the gates, so people who didn't work at the Park could be invited.

'There was a certain camaraderie about it all. There weren't many there, but the section did grow quite considerably. We must have had up to twenty people on each shift.'

The ISK Section was expanding and was now too big for the Cottage so it was moved into Elmer's School alongside the section dealing with the more basic German secret service codes. A number of WAAFs were added to the section to operate modified Typex machines designed to simulate the Abwehr Enigma. They set them up to the keys worked out by Jean and the other girls and typed out the German message on strips of sticky tape, just like the Hut 6 Decoding Room.

'When we thought we had the right answer the girls would set up the machines and hopefully if we'd done our job properly they would get the answers coming up. It was then sent to the translators next door. I don't think I ever knew any more than that. The security in the Park was absolutely unbelievably tight.'

Dilly spent most of his time at Courns Wood, working with Margaret on a top-secret project which not even Mavis knew anything about, but he did come in occasionally to see them, and once when Jean was going to see her parents for some leave, he offered to drop her off on his way home.

'I had one hair-raising journey with him when he volunteered to drop me off at Wendover. He drove half the time with no hands on the wheel because he was explaining various things. Fortunately, Mrs Dilly was in the car. In the end she said, "Dilly, you really ought to put one hand on the steering wheel."'

Margaret was seriously ill herself for several months in the first half of 1942 and Peter Twinn and Keith Batey were brought in from Hut 8 and Hut 6 to bolster the codebreaking capability in the ISK Section. While Keith had deliberately ignored Mavis's attempt to draw him into picking up her pencil when they were working on the Italian naval Enigma, romance blossomed once they were working together full-time.

But, like many of the young men at Bletchley, Keith felt that he should be taking a more active part in the war. There was undoubtedly pressure on the young men. They had friends who were on the front line, who had no idea why Keith and their like had safe jobs in the countryside, away from the fighting and the bombing. The woman who provided Keith's first billet had even demanded an assurance that he wasn't a conscientious objector before she was prepared to let him into her house.

Keith told Gordon Welchman bluntly that there was no reason not to let the young men who wanted to do their bit go off to war. Women were perfectly capable of breaking codes. Mavis, Margaret and Joan Clarke had all shown that, and many of Dilly's Girls were doing the routine work without any idea of mathematical theory or how the code worked, most of them without ever having seen an Enigma machine. Why not allow the women to get on with it and let the fit young men play their part in the war?

His bosses at Bletchley blanched at the idea of one of their leading Enigma codebreakers putting himself at risk of being captured and giving away the Enigma secret, but there was a compromise when Keith agreed to join the Fleet

Air Arm, the Royal Navy's air service, rather than the RAF; if he was shot down it would always be over the sea, with an expectation that he would die. Perhaps understandably, Mavis never found this particularly reassuring.

Meanwhile, Dilly's condition was deteriorating. It was clear that he was living on borrowed time and in between his visits to the ISK Section, Mavis occasionally went over to Courns Wood in an official car to seek his advice on what they were doing. On one occasion, she spent the weekend there.

'My most enduring memory of Dilly is staying at Courns Wood in his last spring. He had invited me over to see the "loveliest of trees, the cherry" now in full bloom under the guest bedroom. He was still passionate about trees but he could no longer do the strenuous planting he so loved to do. I just helped him shake pine cone seeds into tobacco tins for scattering.'

Keith joined the Fleet Air Arm in June 1942, but he wasn't taking any chances and before he left he proposed to Mavis, who agreed to marry him and had to confess to Dilly that she was engaged to a mathematician.

'Although Dilly congratulated me heartily, he asked me if I knew that mathematicians as a breed were not very imaginative. I reassured him that this one was all right. When I showed Olive my engagement ring and said I had chosen it myself, she told me that Dilly had bought hers himself, as he thought that was what the bridegroom was supposed to do. By the tone in her voice, I rather detected that she too would have preferred to be in on the choice.'

Keith's initial training didn't go well. On his first solo flight, he came in to land so low that the examiners had to dive to the ground to avoid being decapitated. They passed him, largely because they were desperate for new pilots, but they expressed some reservations. He had to go to Canada to do his full flying training in November 1942 so Mavis and he got married at Marylebone Registry Office, with Peter Twinn as Keith's best man.

'Dilly sent us a lovely wedding present and said that if the Muse hadn't left him he would have composed my wedding hymn.'

Dilly's wedding present was a silver condiment set engraved with the letters ISK. There was a brief three-day honeymoon in the Lake District, which was interrupted by Keith's brother Herbert, who came down from Carlisle to see them. Mavis was not at all happy when Keith spent most of one of their precious three days together playing chess with his brother.

After the honeymoon, Keith sailed for Canada. The U-boats were concentrating on sinking ships sailing along the east coast of America but Hut 8 at this time still hadn't broken the Shark Enigma, so Mavis relied on the girls in the Naval Section to keep her informed of his ship's progress across the Atlantic and safe arrival in Newfoundland.

'Shortly afterwards, Dilly was admitted to University College Hospital and when I visited him his brother Evoe, who was editor of *Punch*, was by his bedside and they were roaring with laughter composing Dilly's last words.'

Dilly went home to Courns Wood to die. He got out of

bed when a representative of the King came to appoint him as a Companion of the Order of St Michael and St George, the traditional award given to members of the intelligence services whose work is so secret it can barely be acknowledged. Dilly was adamant that it was for Mavis and his 'girls' as much as for him.

'Dilly insisted on getting dressed to receive the emissary from Buckingham Palace and typically he sent the decoration to ISK with a touching note saying it was really meant for us. It was heartening to know that he regarded ISK and what he called the "Cottage tradition" as the fulfilment of his career.'

Dilly died at Courns Wood on 27 February 1943, aged fifty-eight, and was buried in the woodland he had lovingly nurtured.

The breaking of the Abwehr Enigma codes and the messages that continued to pour out of the ISK Section provided the intelligence officers running the Double Cross operation with complete confidence that they controlled all the Nazi agents sent to Britain, and that all the false intelligence they were feeding back to the Germans was believed.

This allowed them to take the operation one stage further in the run-up to D-Day, supplying coordinated intelligence from all the double agents to create a completely false picture of a fictitious First United States Army Group, based in southeast England, which was to lead the main thrust of the Allied invasion against the area around Calais. The aim was to persuade the Germans to keep most of their troops near to Calais and give the real landings in Normandy an easier run.

The false intelligence was supplied to the Germans as individual pieces of information from a number of different double agents, which the Abwehr would be able to put together themselves with each agent seeming to back up what the others said.

The most important of the Double Cross agents used in this 'deception operation' was a Spaniard called Juan Pujol García, codenamed Garbo. He claimed in his reports to the Germans to be running a network of twenty-seven agents across the UK, including a Swiss businessman in Bootle who reported 'drunken orgies and slack morals in amusement centres' in Liverpool, and a Venezuelan in Glasgow who claimed Clydeside dockers would 'do anything for a litre of wine'. When the Swiss businessman died of cancer, his widow took his place. The Venezuelan also ran agents in Scotland, one of them a communist who thought he was spying for Moscow. Garbo's mistress, a secretary in the War Cabinet, slept with army officers to gather valuable pillow talk. All of these people, including the mistress, were complete fantasy – none of his agents actually existed. Indeed, his claims were so incredible that it would have been impossible to imagine the Germans believing anything he said if it were not for the ISK Section's ability to read the messages encoded on the Abwehr Enigmas.

In the early hours of D-Day, 6 June 1944, as Allied troops poured across the English Channel, Garbo tried repeatedly to warn Berlin that they were on their way to

Normandy. It was deliberately too late for the Germans to do anything about it, but ensured they still saw Garbo as their most reliable spy.

Three days later, with Allied forces struggling to break through the German defences, and two German armoured divisions on their way to Normandy, Garbo sent his most important message. His agents were reporting troops massed in ports in East Anglia and Kent. The Normandy landings were a diversion. The real landings were to be in Calais as the Germans had always believed. Garbo's warning went straight to Hitler, who ordered the two armoured divisions back to Calais to defend against what he expected to be the main invasion thrust. This decision ensured the success of the Allied invasion. Had the two divisions continued to Normandy, the Allies might well have been thrown back into the sea.

Brigadier Bill Williams, the officer in charge of intelligence for the British troops at D-Day, said the deception would not have been possible had Dilly and his girls not broken the 'Spy Enigma'. By the time the troops began wading ashore in Normandy, Dilly had been dead for more than fifteen months, but he had played a vital part in the success of the D-Day landings. By trusting Mavis, Margaret and the rest of Dilly's Girls to follow his instructions and break the codes, he had achieved what was quite possibly the most important codebreaking success of the Second World War.

8

The World's First Electronic Computer

The two-year period leading up to D-Day saw a huge increase in the number of people working at Bletchley and the Bombe outstations, and with every available young man needed for the fighting, the vast majority of the new recruits were women. In June 1942, there were 1,900 people working at Bletchley Park of whom two-thirds were female. By D-Day, 6 June 1944, there were just under 8,000 people at Bletchley with three-quarters of them women.

Even in the sections dealing with the Enigma codes, the number of women rose dramatically. By June 1944, there were more than 500 people in Hut 6 breaking the German army and air force Enigma codes and 460 reporting the intelligence in Hut 3. Hut 8 was substantially smaller, with 150 people, in part because the Americans were now doing a lot of the work on the German naval Enigma, but Hut 4, the Naval Section, had 950 people, of whom fewer than a hundred were men.

For security reasons the sections working on Enigma continued to use their original titles, even though they were now in the new brick- and concrete-built blocks. People had become comfortable in the old wooden huts and were not necessarily happy to move. Sally Norton complained of transferring 'from Hut 4, which we loved, into a horrible concrete building'. Mair Thomas had similar feelings.

'In all truth our new block was a bit of a dump. Even though it was brand new and built for the new workers it was grim and functional. It felt a bit like working in a factory or a battery farm. I didn't like the inconvenience of moving; it was disorientating. The old hut, with all its shabbiness, was familiar and settled.'

The facilities for women also increased. A local hairdresser set up a salon in the Park charging a shilling (5p) for a trim and three shillings and sixpence (17½p) for a shampoo and set. With too many of the billets having limited washing facilities, a bath house was built beside Block F and, amid concern that the lack of natural light in the new blocks was taking its toll on the health of some of the young women, a 'Sun Ray Clinic' was set up.

Commander Denniston had successfully established the idea that Bletchley should have first call on mathematicians, and to a certain extent linguists, in the early years of the war, but with far more fighting going on around the world there was now an increasing need for men on the front line and good reason why German and Japanese linguists were needed in other parts of the war effort. Women had to make up the bulk of the staff and even the four sections breaking the Enigma messages and reporting on them to

London and to front line commanders were increasingly involving women in work that during the early years of the war had been the exclusive preserve of the men.

Hut 3 got around the Civil Service regulations on women working alongside men on the night shift by setting up an entirely female reporting shift for the Watch, who carried out all of the immediate intelligence reporting. Both Hut 3 and Hut 6 brought in large numbers of army intelligence analysts, the majority of them women, and Hut 6 split the main codebreaking section, the Machine Room, into two. The Hut 6 codebreakers who did the initial work looking for ways into the Enigma codes formed a new section, which like its Hut 3 equivalent was called the Watch. The Machine Room was turned into a completely female section, giving some of the women from the old Decoding Room and a number of smaller sections of Hut 6 some of the codebreaking work. The women taken out of the Decoding Room were largely replaced by female Typex operators who typed the messages out mechanically and had no need to understand German.

The men on the Watch worked out the cribs and passed them through a hatch into the Machine Room where a female codebreaker worked out the menus for the Bombes, liaised with the Wrens running the Bombes, and tested out the settings thrown up by them on captured Enigma machines.

Ann Williamson was one of a very few female mathematicians in the country at that time. When she'd said at school that she wanted to specialise in that area her headmistress had told her she couldn't because 'mathematics

is not a ladylike subject'. Fortunately, Ann's parents over-
ruled the headmistress and eventually Ann earned a place
reading mathematics at Lady Margaret Hall, Oxford.

'When I went up to Oxford in 1940, there were five
women in the whole university who were reading maths
that year. We were very scarce.'

After completing her degree, the Oxford University
appointments board sent Ann and another of the five
female maths graduates to interviews at Bletchley Park and
a few weeks later they received letters from the Foreign
Office appointing them as temporary assistants at a salary
of £150 a year and telling them to report to Bletchley. The
other girl joined Hut 8; Ann went into the new all-female
Machine Room.

'We had to go through the Watch to get to the Machine
Room and just by the door connecting the two was a
table with pieces of paper laid out on which people in the
Watch had written some of the jumbled nonsense that
came through the air waves and then underneath they'd
written what they thought it might be saying in German.
We would pick up one of these pieces of paper and make
a menu, connecting these letters we received to the letters
they should have been saying. I loved that work making
menus. It was very like doing crosswords, joining a chain
of letters.'

The menus were sent through to the Wrens coordinating
the work that the various Bombe outstations would carry
out via a Lamson pressurised air communications system.
The menu was put into a canister which was then inserted
into a tube connecting the Machine Room with the Bombe

Control Room. A partial vacuum in the tube system drew the canister in and routed it through to the Bombe Control Room. Ann and the other girls called it the 'spit and suck' because the pressurised air system sucked the capsule in and 'spat it out' at the other end.

'The Wrens working on the Bombes would set them up and then telephone us when they got a stop, which would be the position at which the Bombe stopped where all the chains on your menu were accurate.'

The women in the Machine Room then set up an Enigma machine with the right rotors and settings thrown up by the Bombe and typed in the letters of the message to see if the letters lighting up on top of the Enigma machine produced German text. If they did, then the settings would be passed through to the Decoding Room where the women set up their modified Typex machines and typed out all the messages from that particular German network. Ann and her fellow female codebreakers had a far more interesting job than any of the women in Hut 6 had enjoyed before.

'The most important code for us was the Red. There were ten or so of us working in the Machine Room. It sounds much more complicated than we found it at the time. It was fascinating, all these messages coming out in German. I loved it.'

The expansion of the whole process into what was effectively a factory production line, impossible without the increased numbers the women provided, was essential if the codebreakers were to keep track of German troops during the invasion of Europe, but by now Bletchley had broken a code that was even more complex. The messages they decoded would tell Allied commanders precisely what Hitler and his generals planned to do next.

All the main front-line command posts were linked to Hitler's command posts in Berlin and Rastenberg in Poland by teleprinter links on which the messages were automatically encoded by the Lorenz SZ40 device. There was an SZ40 between the teleprinter and the transmitter and another at the other end between the receiver and the teleprinter. The operator at one end simply typed the German message in, the SZ40 encrypted it, and the transmitter sent out the encoded message. At the other end the encoded message passed through another SZ40 which decoded it, and the message then typed up automatically in plain German text on another teleprinter.

The codebreakers gave the Lorenz system the code-name Tunny, after the fish more commonly known as tuna. Each of the teleprinter links between Hitler and the various generals on the front line was given the name of a different fish. The two most important ones for British commanders were between Hitler and the German commander in France, Field Marshal Gerd von Rundstedt, which Bletchley codenamed Jellyfish, and the link between Hitler and Field Marshal Albert Kesselring, the German commander in Italy, which they called Bream.

The Lorenz SZ40 had twelve wheels, ten to encipher the message (paired in two separate rows of five) and two drive wheels. The movement of the second row of wheels was highly complex, making it difficult to break. But in

1942, in an extraordinary piece of codebreaking, John Tiltman and Bill Tutte, a recently recruited chemistry and mathematics graduate, did just that and two new sections were set up to work on it.

The first section, run by Max Newman and called the Newmanry, worked out how the first row of wheels were set and how they rotated. The second section, led by Ralph Tester and called the Testery, used the stream of letters produced by the Newmanry to work out the action of the second set of wheels and decode the actual messages.

Newman, who had been Alan Turing's tutor at Cambridge, realised that the work in his section could be done much faster by the sort of 'computing machinery' that his former student had already envisaged building. This didn't yet exist. It was just a series of ideas in Turing's mind. But Newman put his ideas to the head post office research engineer Tommy Flowers and explained precisely what the 'computing machinery' needed to do. By the end of 1943 Mr Flowers and his team had produced Colossus, the world's first electronic digital computer, an astonishing, ground-breaking achievement that, because of the secrecy surrounding the work of the codebreakers, would go unrecognised for decades. Colossus did not break the messages. This still had to be done by hand. But it made the process of working out the settings of the first row of wheels far quicker.

The encoded German teleprinter messages were inter-cepted at Knockholt, near Sevenoaks in Kent, and printed out on perforated paper teleprinter tape. The tape of the messages was run through Colossus, which read it electronically and worked out the wheel settings and the way in which the wheels moved. It needed two people to operate it, quite aside from the codebreakers who were working out *how* it should be operated. Given the success of using the Wrens to operate the Bombe machines, it was no surprise that they turned to them to operate Colossus.

Marigold Philips was born in Etwall, near Derby, to members of what was then known as the 'County Set'. Her father was the managing director of a Manchester warehousing company and while the family had no aristocratic links they regarded themselves, and were regarded locally, as country gentry.

'If you owned property you were somebody in those days. We lived in a medium-sized country house where the horses and dogs were much more interesting than the people. I was the odd one out in that I wanted to think and have ideas whereas most young female members of the country gentry just wanted a rich husband and more horses.'

Although Marigold regarded her mother and father as good parents, it was not a very close relationship. While children were not regarded as being as low down in the scale of importance as servants, they were certainly kept out of the way most of the time, minded by nursemaids when they weren't being taught to read and write by their nanny or later given more extensive education by a governess.

'Children were something you had that lived somewhere else in the house and were expected to grow up and conform. We weren't the apple of anyone's eye. Children were children. Speak when you're spoken to. Live your own life in the nursery. I had a nanny and then a governess before I went away to school, which I was longing to do.'

Marigold went to Downe House School at Cold Ash in Berkshire as a boarder. It was a very good school and at the time emphasised the need for 'low living and high thinking' – a total change from what she was used to at home.

'It's now seen as very trendy, but it was then seen as a very intellectual school. We were serious-minded, gently feminist and expected to have careers.'

During the school holidays, Marigold's mother made sure she and her sister were tightly chaperoned. They were only allowed to go out with young men if the cook went with them, so they became quite adroit at getting round the restrictions.

'It was terribly easy. You dropped the cook off at the nearest pub, gave her some money for a drink and picked her up on the way back. But the interesting twist is that in those days at sixteen or seventeen we didn't really know what we were being chaperoned for, because we didn't know what the hidden dangers with young men were.'

It wasn't until she went up to Oxford to read English Literature at Somerville College, then an all-women college, that she learned the facts of life.

'I was sexually ignorant and a young don's wife put me right on certain things. She was appalled to find that I didn't know. This was typical of young girls from our privileged but fairly un-intellectual background.'

When she finished her 'wartime degree', restricted to

two years so the students could leave and contribute to the war effort, Marigold's mother told her to join the Wrens. It was an entirely pragmatic social decision and, despite having been to university, Marigold was still not twenty-one and so was given no choice.

'My mother thought it was time I came off my intellectual high horse and the Wrens were thought to be where young ladies were more likely to meet suitable husbands, i.e. naval officers, heaven help us.'

After three weeks at Mill Hill scrubbing floors to make sure she was willing to follow orders, Marigold was interviewed and asked if she liked crossword puzzles – she didn't. How about maths? She insisted she was hopeless at it. They didn't seem to care. She was sent first to Eastcote for a period of induction into the world of codebreaking and then, in August 1943, to Bletchley to work in the Newmanry.

'I realised subsequently that they didn't give a damn about what your qualifications were, if you were a nice young girl from a decent family you were not likely to rat on them.'

Dorothy du Boisson, a 23-year-old from Edmonton, north London, arrived a couple of months before Marigold and was given a talk by Max Newman on what the work involved.

'Mr Newman was a very quiet man, reserved and not at ease with girls. He walked up and down in front of us with his eyes on the ground, talking about a machine with twelve wheels. When he had gone we were none the wiser. Later we discovered that he thought we had been told what the section did. Mr Newman decreed that everyone, except himself, be called by their first name. This was a wonderful idea. At once we were a team.'

Maggie Broughton-Thompson, an eighteen-year-old vicar's daughter from Brewood in Staffordshire, joined the Wrens straight from school. She'd been due to go to Mill Hill to do her basic training but a doodlebug had hit it, putting it briefly out of action, and she was sent instead to Tullichewan Castle.

'I got the impression practically everyone in my draft was already earmarked to go to Bletchley because we certainly had no choice and we had no particular interview or anything. We were just told we were all going to the same place and they couldn't tell us where it was or anything about it because we simply weren't allowed to know. So that was it.'

Maggie worked on the computer and also in a long room where the messages coming in from Knockholt printed out on perforated paper teleprinter tape and were prepared for use on Colossus. Two identical tapes would be spliced together with glue, using a heated clamp, to make a loop which would run through the computer repeatedly.

'The messages were transferred in duplicate. You had to first of all make sure that there were no mistakes, that the two tapes were identical, and then however long or short the message was, the two ends were spliced together in a machine that sort of stamped them together so that they didn't come apart.'

There were two Wren registrars working in the Registry

Office, keeping a record of every tape that came in, the time that it was run through Colossus, how long the run took and where exactly every tape was located after being run.

Jean Thompson was just nineteen when she was posted to Bletchley in 1944 to work on Colossus; she spent most of her time working on the computer itself. Two Wrens would operate the machine under the direction of a duty officer, one of the codebreakers, all of whom were male.

'If the pattern of the wheels was already known you put that up at the back of the machine on a pinboard. The pins were bronze, brass or copper with two feet and there were double holes the whole way down the board for cross or dot impulses to put up the wheel pattern. Then you put the paper tape on round the wheels with a join in it so it formed a complete circle.'

The number of wheels used depended on how long the tape was. The tape was placed behind the computer's photo-electric cell and held secure by a clip, then the movable pulley wheels were adjusted to make sure the tape was taut.

'At the front there were switches and plugs. After you'd set the thing you could do a letter count with the switches. You would make the runs for the different wheels to get the scores out, which would print out on the electro-matic typewriter. We were looking for a score above the random, and one that was sufficiently good you'd hope was the correct setting. When it got tricky, the duty officer would suggest different runs to do.'

Marigold worked in both the Registry Office and on

Colossus, which generated a lot of heat and smelled of hot oil. It was a mindless task that didn't require either mathematics or an intellect. They had to log every tape and how long it had taken to run the job.

'It was very hot and we wore our blouses with the sleeves rolled up. But we were young and it was the war. We didn't give a stuff about that sort of thing.'

They also knew that they were doing something very valuable to the war effort. Mr Newman held regular briefings for the Wrens to make sure they knew the importance of doing the work as quickly as possible and that they were actually having an effect on the war.

'He had the imagination to realise that young people would work better if they were kept informed – which we were, amazingly – of some of the effects of what our spying had led to – because it was a form of spying. Once a fortnight, he would give us a résumé of what was happening.'

Perhaps most surprising of all, given the tight security at Bletchley, with no one allowed to know what other sections at the Park were doing, Mr Newman didn't restrict himself to the successes produced by the breaking of the Newmanry and the Testery, even talking about the successes resulting from Hut 8's breaking of the naval Enigma.

'He told us at Christmas 1943 about the sinking of the *Scharnhorst* being directly related to Bletchley. I'll always remember being told about this, also from time to time about the sinking of German U-boats. We were given quite specific information but I don't think there was any thought that we would disclose it. He would talk to us and trust us. He was a rather remarkable person and he treated us with great respect even though we were just doing this rather mindless task as we saw it.'

They were billeted in Woburn Abbey. Marigold's 'cabin' was in one of a number of wooden huts in the parkland around the house.

'They were called cabins because we had to speak navy talk all the time. We went in through the front door where there was a very fierce woman called the regulating officer, a terrifying blonde lady.'

Maggie slept in the old maids' quarters in the attic along with a number of other girls from the Newmanry. They were squeezed into double bunks which had wire-mesh bases that you could feel through the very thin mattress.

'It was bitterly cold in winter and diabolically hot in summer. They could just about fit in four double-decker bunks so there were eight of us squashed in, with very little space. We all worked on the same watch, which was essential. If you had night watches, you were asleep during the day – you couldn't have people rushing in and out. We all got on very well together. The cabin became our little social group.'

There were four watches, A, B, C and D, working round the clock. When Marigold first arrived in the late summer of 1943, before the arrival of Colossus, there were just seventeen Wrens in the Newmanry. By mid-1944, with one Colossus computer up and running and several more on the way, there were eighty-six Wrens there with around twenty on each watch. A week of nights was followed by a week of evening shifts, then a week of days and then a week when the members of the watch filled in on other shifts and had the weekend off, during which they would go home or take trips to London.

Marigold used to go to London to meet up with friends from Oxford, all of whom seemed to have had more of their wits about them. They hadn't been pushed by their mothers into the Wrens and were now doing 'interesting things' at the Foreign Office.

'We would go in twos and threes to the theatre or to have dinner with some sad brother or boyfriend, which was the height of glamour. Of course, we fancied men like mad but there was a definite cut-off point. We were told very early on, in my mother's words, "no man will marry a girl who is shop-soiled", a horrible image, but it worked. Most of us were virgins when we married.'

The trips involved quick-change operations from Marigold's naval uniform at the next station on from Bletchley on the slow train to London.

'I clearly remember getting out in my Wren uniform with a little bag, going into the cowshed, changing my clothes and putting my uniform in the manger, then catching the next train up to London in my glad-rags. When we got back we would change back into our uniform, roll up the evening dress and stuff it in something and arrive back at work as a Wren.'

They weren't allowed to stay away overnight; if they had, they would have been deemed to be 'adrift', another uniquely naval expression, in this case for being absent without leave, and they would have been hauled before the regulating officer.

'I was longing to be asked, "Where were you when

you were adrift?" so that I could say, "Clinging to a buoy, ma'am." It would have been so wonderful, but I never got the chance unfortunately.'

Once the settings and rotation of the first row of Lorenz wheels were worked out in the Newmanry, the Testery took over, breaking the messages by hand using pencil and paper. Once they had cracked them and knew the complete settings of the Tunny machine, they were passed through to Room 27, where ATS operators used teleprinters linked to Tunny 'emulators'. The ATS staff pressed buttons to enter the settings for each of the Tunny wheels on the emulator and then typed out the encoded message on the teleprinter. If the settings had been worked out properly and the message typed in correctly, German text printed out.

Helen Pollard, one of the ATS teleprinter operators, had been working as a typist in Fleet Street (then the base for all Britain's major newspapers) when war broke out and she was called up. She worked as an intercept operator in Trowbridge, Wiltshire, during the early years of the war but in the summer of 1942 was picked out for Bletchley and sent to work for Major Ralph Tester in the Testery, ending up in Room 27, working the teleprinters and Tunny emulators.

'Even without knowing the language it was easy to recognise German, and just as easy to see that gibberish was coming out when something went wrong. This happened when a letter was missed out, or one was typed that wasn't there. The gentle clack of the machines as they operated became a background to our working lives. The work never got tedious. There was something about the atmosphere at Bletchley Park that generated an all-pervading excitement.'

Helen fell in love and got married in August 1943 to a young airman, but he was killed ten weeks later. 'The whole section grieved for me. Peter Hilton, a very sweet man, brought me the best and clearest message he could find, which would give me no trouble to type. It was his way of bringing me comfort.'

The run-up to D-Day in the Newmanry was dominated by the need to get ready for the arrival of a new improved Colossus and to hone their skills so that every task was carried out as swiftly and efficiently as possible. The intelligence the codebreakers in the Testery were producing was sent out via Hut 3, like the reports from the German army and air force Enigma messages. Everyone at Bletchley knew that once the invasion of Europe began, the slightest delay in getting the intelligence to the right people could result in the loss of lives. But the social life of the Wrens was dominated by what Marigold and her colleagues saw as the section's 'great romance'.

Odette Murray, the daughter of a Surrey doctor, had worked in the Home Ambulance Service throughout the Blitz, a harrowing but rewarding task. But after having to have her tonsils removed she was told she shouldn't return to working on the ambulances, so she joined the Wrens. Odette was very keen on the idea of being a Wren and travelling to exotic places, so she was extremely disappointed to be sent to Bletchley.

'I wanted to be a boat's crew, I wanted to be going out to places like Colombo. I didn't want to be stuck in the Midlands at all. We turned up at Bletchley Park where we were taught to be touch-typists, still not knowing what it was all about, and eventually got into the Newmanry, it was just starting up. I think at the beginning it was just Max.'

When Odette arrived Mr Newman was working in Hut 11, while the Testery was in the mansion, but in November 1943, the two 'Tunny' sections moved into the newly built Block F and a number of other codebreakers joined the Newmanry, including Shaun Wylie, who at thirty was now a veteran and one of the older, more senior, men in the section.

Odette was not only one of the first Wrens to arrive in the Newmanry, at twenty-five she was slightly older than the other girls and as a result was put in charge of one of the watches; Shaun was her duty officer, the codebreaker who oversaw their work.

'He was my boss. I was head of a watch and I was given instructions by Shaun and, still not having the remotest idea what I was doing, I worked with a slide rule, produced a lot of figures and gave it on to the next person, who gave it on to the next person and eventually it was run on a tape on Colossus. But we really didn't know what it was about.'

Odette also couldn't understand the younger Wrens' fascination with Shaun. They were swooning over him, telling her how wonderful he was all the time. As if she cared.

'The other Wrens thought he was absolutely wonderful:

"Oh, Mr Wylie this, oh, Mr Wylie that." I couldn't see what they saw in him. I didn't think much of him. However, he thought something of me.'

They began going out, spending a lot of time walking in the grounds of Woburn Abbey. Shaun would cycle down there on their days off to meet Odette.

'The abbey is a huge, imposing building. There's an enormous great triangular pediment right up at the very, very top, very high up, and I used to go leaping across two-foot, three-foot chasms so that I could sit on the top of this to watch Shaun on his bicycle coming up the drive. It was one hell of a climb.'

The other regular place where they would do their 'courting' was a pub, the Bedford Arms.

'The wonderful walks we had in Woburn Park. Most of our courting was in Woburn Park and the Bedford Arms, where there was an old woman who was . . . I suppose you would call her a waitress. We used to call her droopy drawers. You could always see her pants hanging down under her dress.'

Despite being the watch leader, Odette had no more idea what she was doing in technical terms than Marigold, Jean or Maggie.

'I knew we were getting something out but I didn't really know what the something was. When Shaun tried to explain to me exactly what my contribution had been in a successful thing, I just didn't understand. I'm not a mathematician. I'm not a linguist. I'm just somebody who's given instructions and does little funny calculations with a slide rule, and bingo. A few days later a smiling

Shaun comes in. I don't know what my contribution is but OK, satisfactory.'

They were married in the early spring of 1944 ahead of the ban on travel introduced for D-Day, but the Wren officers were unhappy that Odette and Shaun would be working together and tried to get him moved out of the Newmanry. Eventually, a compromise was agreed whereby he was never allowed to supervise Odette's watch. They were billeted together in the Swan Hotel in Woburn Sands, which also didn't go down well with the Wren officers.

'It was a blasted nuisance. I rather think that they'd expected me back at Woburn, I know I was given a real bottle. I think I slightly blotted my copybook by losing my leave pass when we had been on our honeymoon, turned up twenty-four hours late or something.'

The extent of the intelligence provided by the teleprinter links broken with the help of Colossus and the Wrens was extraordinary. The Jellyfish teleprinter link between von Rundstedt's headquarters near Paris and Berlin carried all the conversations between the German commander in France and Hitler, including von Rundstedt's plans for how to defend against the impending Allied invasion, and which plans Hitler had ordered him to change, often leaving weak points that could be exploited by Allied commanders. Jellyfish also gave extensive details of the German defensive positions and the strengths and capabilities of the 1.4 million German troops waiting for the invasion. Most importantly of all, it confirmed that Hitler himself had been completely fooled by the Double Cross operation and was convinced that the Allies' main invasion force would come ashore around Calais rather than in Normandy.

On the morning of 6 June 1944, as Allied forces came ashore in Normandy, the bosses at Bletchley Park were very well aware that some of the young men working there would be wondering whether they shouldn't be fighting alongside their friends and relatives, who were now thrust into the thick of battle. Eric Jones, the head of Hut 3, told his staff that the work Bletchley was doing might not be so dangerous but it was just as important to the war effort. There was 'no back-stage organisation that has done more for past Allied operations and Allied plans for this assault; and none that can contribute more to the development of the invasion once the bloody battles for the beaches have been won'.

The extraordinary intelligence produced by the Tunny and Enigma sections ahead of D-Day was unprecedented in its scale, saving countless Allied lives. But initially, the panicky reaction of some of the German forces caused problems in Hut 6, because the Germans were so anxious to report the invasion that they forgot to enter the new day's keys on their Enigma machines. Pamela Draughn came into the Duddery at nine o'clock that morning completely unaware that the invasion had begun.

'I didn't know. I hadn't heard the news before I went into the office and when I got there the night shift was standing there looking absolutely desperate. Wire baskets everywhere full of paper which hadn't decoded.'

The Machine Room had spent most of the night unsure which of the settings the Germans were using was correct, with large numbers of Enigma messages proving impossible to decode. They'd all been sent to the Duddery, where the night shift had become completely overwhelmed.

'At first I really wanted to laugh because it was quite obvious the Germans had got into a complete panic. Obviously the minute they saw the invasion they'd all started reporting it to one another and they'd completely forgotten that they had to change the code. It was absolutely frantic but we could decode them all and eventually we got them all sorted out.'

One of the messages from that night so exemplified the German response and seemed to Pamela to be so poetic that it stuck in her head.

'It said: "We are about to retreat. We can no longer face up to the *von den immer wieder von allen Seiten anfliessenden Feind.*" It means we're fleeing from the from all sides on-flowing enemy!'

From that point onwards, the codebreakers really did feel that they were part of the battle, in much the same way as they had during the North African campaign, and in the same way that Hut 4 and Hut 8 had during the Battle of the Atlantic. Everything was urgent. Everything was important. No one could afford to slacken off. Pamela and her colleagues knew there were too many people, too many lives, depending on them.

'The mood in the hut was always the same. After the invasion it all seemed very much more urgent in a way, as you can imagine. I enjoyed it immensely. You really felt all the time that you were doing something worthwhile.'

Susan Wenham was one of the new female codebreakers

working in the Machine Room. She was quite old at thirty-two, having gone to university late following the death of her mother, and was one of the young women recruited into Hut 6 by Stuart Milner-Barry from Newnham College, Cambridge. She'd started out in the Registry as a 'Blister' and was one of the women transferred to the all-female Machine Room in 1942 in time for the move into Block D, which was far from a major improvement in terms of working conditions.

'Hut 6 was not luxurious; the rooms might not be left when the cleaners came to sweep and the red dust got into our noses and throats; Bovril from the urn was revolting and put me off it forever. Meals in the canteen were adequate if unexciting and there was always salad and, unfailingly, beetroot in small cubes.'

As the Allies began building up a massive foothold in northern France, Hitler became frustrated with the inability of his commanders to find a way to hold back the US and British advance. The Newmanry received a teleprinter message from Hitler ordering his commanders to strike north to the Channel to cut the Allied advance in two and turn the tables on them. It was extraordinarily risky, if not foolhardy, and would have been highly unlikely to succeed even if Bletchley had not been reading Hitler's teleprinter conversations with his generals. Given that Allied commanders were fully aware of the plans, it had no chance of success. But the German generals had no choice but to obey Hitler. Any other route would have been treason and, effectively, suicide. They pressed forward into the Falaise Gap, twenty-five miles south of Caen, and found themselves caught between the advancing US forces and the British and Canadian forces moving in from the north.

Susan was on duty in the Machine Room and in 'the most exciting night' she had at Bletchley found herself working on a long message giving the German plans to try to get out of the Allied trap.

'It was at the time of the Falaise Gap and the Germans were making plans to make their last terrific push to try and get out of the pincer they were in. I was on the night shift and the day shift had had an enormous message.'

The long German Enigma messages had to be sent in sections in an unsuccessful attempt to make it harder to break. The sections were known as *Teile*, the German word for 'parts'.

'It was a ten-*Teile* message, a huge message, and they had managed to break it during the day and it was to say how the Germans were planning to get out of this impasse, and six of the *Teile* came through to us.'

The German generals had realised that they had no chance of obeying Hitler's orders and so rather than lose 300,000 men they decided to withdraw.

Then, during Susan's shift, another six-part message came through in a different code. When the Registry checked it, each part had the same number of groups as in the earlier message that had been broken, so they knew it was exactly the same message in another Enigma army code that hadn't been read before but could now be broken.

'During the night, a very obvious re-encodement of the earlier message came in. We could see that it was a word-for-word re-encodement. So we let Hut 3 know and got all the Bombes cleared. We worked like mad on this thing, creating menus. It was a very tiring business. By morning it was all put through and finished. So that was a very exciting night.'

As the Allied forces moved across France, Belgium and Holland into Germany, more and even better Colossus computers were delivered to Bletchley until in the end there were ten in all. With the German troops largely on the retreat, the Enigma messages became less important. It was the Tunny messages which were producing by far the best intelligence, revealing the increasingly desperate responses of Hitler and his generals. Helen recalled that she and the other girls in the Testery found themselves working nonstop.

'The last stages of the war were hectic. The traffic became almost more than we could cope with. Sometimes, having staggered off duty and dropped exhausted into bed, we were aroused from deep sleep a couple of hours later to return to the Testery and carry on.'

Although Helen had lost her husband in the most tragic of circumstances there was no option for the young widow but to go back to work and get on with life.

'I and many of my friends in the Testery made the most of life. There were some passionate romances. We lived totally in the present, greedy for life and with no thought for the future. We didn't know if there would be a future.'

On days off and even between shifts they would take the train to London. Sometimes, they went to a film in the morning, a theatre matinee in the evening and followed that with dinner and dancing.

'Catching the last train back to Bletchley, we arrived just in time to change into uniform and report for duty, to relieve the girls who had been bashing away at the machines all evening. It was a stimulating, exhausting life.'

On 30 April 1945, with German resistance almost over and Russian troops closing in on his bunker in Berlin, Hitler committed suicide. Then, in the early hours of 7 May 1945, Hut 6 received a message they didn't need to decode. It was from Grand Admiral Dönitz, Commander-in-Chief of the German Navy and Hitler's successor, saying that Germany had surrendered unconditionally. The message was passed to Hut 3, which reported it immediately to London. The contents were known throughout both Hut 6 and Hut 3 almost immediately but none of them said a word to anyone outside their hut. That was the way it was at Bletchley. The news remained a secret even within the Park until it was broadcast later that day on the BBC.

9

The Jappy Waaf

Mary Wisbey's recruitment to Bletchley Park wasn't just like something out of a spy novel. It was the real thing. She'd been due to take up a place at Lady Margaret Hall, Oxford, but to the dismay of her father, a Northamptonshire businessman, she insisted on joining the Women's Auxiliary Air Force. What was the point of going to university when the country was at war? Everyone else was doing something; she should be doing something too. Her father disagreed. He'd served in the First World War, been taken prisoner by the Germans. He knew the war wouldn't end quickly. He wanted Mary to take up the place at Oxford now. She could always join the WAAFs later once she'd got her degree.

But Mary wasn't to be dissuaded. Initially too young to join up, she studied German and French at a language school in the morning and in the afternoon worked in a canteen for servicemen until she reached that all-important age of seventeen and a half and was old enough to join the WAAF.

'We had fifteen days' training at Innsworth, near

Gloucester, and we weren't in uniform.' The Women's Auxiliary Air Force hadn't yet got enough equipment or uniforms. 'After the tenth or eleventh day we got our uniforms. I had no idea at all what I was going to do, I had no qualifications at all; I just was hell-bent on being a WAAF.'

After training and a very brief stint in Coastal Command, Mary was transferred to aircrew selection and sent to Downing College, Cambridge, to study 'the psychology of the interview' under Professor Frederic Bartlett, then one of the world leaders in the field of cognitive psychology, the science of how humans think.

'I rather imagine that already I'd been earmarked for some sort of intelligence work and I think it was Professor Bartlett who was responsible for what followed.'

Mary was called back for a second course in psychology and then given an intriguing set of orders. She was told to go to H. Sichel's, a wine merchants based in Soho, and say a coded phrase to one of the assistants behind the counter.

'I said what I had to say. I was taken to the back of the shop and a button was pressed – a door opened up and closed behind me and I was in a completely different world.'

Herbert Sichel, a member of a family of genuine and very famous wine merchants, had begun working for MI6 before the war, setting up his own wine importers, distinct from the family business, and using it to gather intelligence on Germany and Italy. The various branches of his shops were employed as fronts for MI6 operations and for the recruitment and payment of spies.

'There was a wine shop on one side and then when you went through the door there was a large place full of people, desks and things. I was told to go upstairs and at the top of the stairs there was an office. There was a senior officer sat behind a desk and a row of coloured telephones and he was talking into two different telephones in two different languages.'

Eventually, he put one of the phones down and a short while afterwards ended the other telephone conversation. He then asked Mary some fairly innocuous questions before telling her she would have to go before a full selection board. She was called back to London a couple of weeks later and in a more formal setting sat before a board chaired by a senior RAF officer but made up mostly of people who seemed to be civilians, including at least one woman.

'They were terrifying people, eight or nine of them. The questions were extremely varied. They asked me about French poetry. They asked me about German philosophy. They asked me about all sorts of things but then came that awful question. They asked me what I thought about the art of the Ming dynasty.'

Mary struggled for what to her seemed ages but was probably not much more than ten seconds. She was fed up with all the stupid questions that couldn't possibly have any relevance to what was going on in the war, and for a brief moment the only way out seemed to be flippancy.

'I think it's slightly different from the Ting.'

There was a deathly silence. Everyone seemed to be looking at her as if she was a stupid young girl who didn't understand how serious everything was.

'My answer was so frivolous and ghastly that I thought as soon as I said it, you idiot, what on earth did you say that for? That's put the lid on everything. And then to my great surprise, someone sniggered, and then they all laughed, and the chairman said: "Thank you. That will be all."'

Mary was certain she'd messed it up, but a few weeks later she received a letter ordering her to report to the School of Oriental and African Studies, in the centre of London's Bloomsbury district, to study Japanese. She wasn't the only one. There were six other WAAFs on the same course: Eileen Clarke, Evelyn Curtis, Cicely Naismith, Denise Gifford-Hull, Margaret Brabbs and Peggy Jackson.

They hit it off immediately, seven young women living in London in RAF quarters off Hallam Street, learning Japanese together, testing each other with cards depicting the various Japanese *Kana* syllables on their way to college, to the bemusement of the other passengers on the red No. 14 double-decker bus. The girls had no idea why they were learning Japanese, although the fact that they seemed to be learning only words related to the use of aircraft gave them a clue. But they were young women growing up quickly together. They bonded in an astonishingly inseparable way, calling themselves 'the JappyWaaf', although none of them could quite remember who suggested the title or why.

It was supposed to be a six-month course, but three months in Mary was pulled out, leaving the others behind, and told she was needed urgently. Even then no one told her where she was going. She was just given a railway warrant and told to take a certain train from Euston Station and get off at the third stop. The third stop was Bletchley Junction.

'There was an RAF person on the platform waiting for me. I was taken up to Church Green, put in a hut, given a bed and told that I was to report to Joe Hooper, the head of the Japanese Air Section, in Block F the next day.'

Britain had been breaking Japanese codes since the 1920s, first in Shanghai, then Hong Kong, and from August 1939 in Singapore. Most of the codes were broken initially in England by John Tiltman, the head of the Bletchley Park Military Section, a man so bright that he'd been offered a place at Oxford at the age of thirteen. Tiltman broke the main Japanese army code in September 1938 and the main Japanese naval code JN25 within weeks of its introduction in the summer of 1939. The results were then sent out to Singapore, where they continued breaking the codes on a daily basis using the methods Tiltman had devised.

But initially it was the Japanese diplomatic messages that were more important to Bletchley, and in particular the messages sent by the Japanese ambassador in Berlin, Oshima Hiroshi, who had direct access to Hitler and senior figures within the Nazi regime. Oshima reported back to Tokyo on everything the Germans were doing, using a machine cipher that the Allies codenamed Purple. The British codebreakers hadn't cracked it, but the Americans had, and when they arrived at Bletchley Park in February 1941 to drink sherry with Commander Denniston they brought a Purple machine with them to exchange for the British expertise in breaking the German Enigma codes.

Purple was one of the US codebreakers' greatest contributions to the Anglo-American cooperation in breaking the wartime codes. It allowed Bletchley to read all the top-secret messages between Japan's embassies around the world and Tokyo, most importantly Oshima's reports from Berlin on what Hitler planned to do next.

When the Japanese invaded Malaya in December 1941, the British Far Eastern codebreakers had to flee Singapore, moving first to Colombo in Ceylon (now Sri Lanka) and then, in April 1942 to Kilindini, near Mombasa, in what is now Kenya but was then known as British East Africa. From 1941 onwards they were supported by a number of Wrens. Some intercepted the messages, others helped in the codebreaking process or analysed the Japanese communications to gather intelligence. The Wrens also operated Hollerith electro-mechanical data-processing machines, precursors of the computer. The Hollerith machines sorted cards on which data was punched using a system of rectangular holes. Operated almost entirely by women, they were a key part of the codebreaking process at Bletchley itself, initially in Hut 7 and from late 1942 in the newly built Block C. Marjorie Halcrow, a 22-year-old graduate from Aberdeen University, was one of those working there.

'The cards were punched up on a machine about the size of a typewriter. There was a room containing about twenty or thirty of them called the punch room where girls copied the coded messages onto these punch cards. The main room contained much larger machines – about the size of a small piano – called the sorting machines, which could read the cards and sort the hundreds of thousands of messages into different categories. There were loads of sorters and there were collating machines that were even larger. The whole department was filled with machinery. It was a very noisy place, banging on all night and day.'

Once the Hollerith machines moved into Block C, a Japanese Naval Section was set up in Hut 7 under Hugh Foss. It was the first of what would become a large number of dedicated Japanese sections. Hugh's team worked on all the naval codes in close collaboration with Kilindini.

Hugh Foss was a brilliant codebreaker who'd done some pioneering work on Enigma long before Dilly Knox took it on. But he had a somewhat quirky personality and his cousin Elizabeth Browning, who also worked in the Japanese Naval Section, recalled that this eccentricity was vividly reflected in his household arrangements. His wife Alison struggled to cope with their two small children and managing the house so Hugh would go home every day at half past four to put the children to bed and cook the evening meal.

'An example of their *modus vivendi* was the highly complicated arrangement for washing-up (dreamed up, needless to say, by Hugh). Every article was supposed to be washed in a particular order – saucers first (as least polluted by human lips); then teaspoons; then side plates; then pudding plates; soup bowls; main course plates; knives; glasses; cups; forks; pudding and soup spoons; and finally saucepans. As these were usually stacked on the floor the dogs were a great help.'

While the theory behind this might have been logical to Hugh's highly ordered mind, housework wasn't seen as a high priority in the Foss household and there were usually several days' worth of plates and dishes piled up in and around the sink.

'If one tried to help there would be shrieks of: "Oh, you mustn't do the cups yet, saucers first." There was also in theory some weird arrangement so that things Hugh was supposed to put away were located at distances appropriate to his great height and long arms, while Alison, who was small and dumpy, had a shorter range. But in practice things ended up pretty well anywhere.'

The Japanese Naval Section included a number of Wrens like Rosemary Calder, who worked in the Traffic Analysis Section run by the Cambridge historian Sir John Plumb.

'I was interviewed by Jack Plumb who told me "we analyse traffic". I had no idea what this meant. I had this picture in my mind of people sat on camp stools by the side of the road counting lorries.'

Angus Wilson, later a famous novelist, was in charge of the actual room in which Rosemary worked. He was openly homosexual in a way which would never have been allowed in most top-secret establishments in wartime Britain.

'Angus was a great darling who spoiled us all and we spoiled him in return. He called us all "ducky" and he had this special friend called Bentley Bridgewater who later went on to become Secretary of the British Museum. Angus was brilliant but crazy. He'd had at least one nervous breakdown before I got there and was still going to Oxford to see a psychiatrist. But he was very good-natured most of the time and if he started getting agitated, we would just give him a copy of *Vogue* or *Tatler* and he could go off and sit down by the lake flicking through it and come back as happy as a sandboy.'

The entire section was very egalitarian; everyone was treated as if they had as much intellectual capability as anyone else and encouraged to use their own initiative.

'Any of us could do any of the jobs in the office. It was a very democratic place, Wrens mixed up with civilians. We might as well have not been in uniform. We were having a marvellous time. It was like being back at college.'

When Olive Humble was called up at the beginning of 1943 she wanted to join the Wrens but she was sent to the Foreign Office and packed off to Bletchley to work for Hugh Foss. After leaving school, Olive had worked in an insurance office in the City and, like the majority of the young women at Bletchley, had never left home before.

'I arrived at Bletchley Park and, to my great consternation, was escorted to the billeting office by an armed soldier. I was parcelled off to a Commander Thatcher, a fierce naval man who put the fear of God into me. He informed me that from then on I would not be allowed to leave the Park other than through death or disablement, that if I said one word of what I or anyone else was doing, even to my nearest and dearest, I would get thirty years without the option. He stood over me while I digested the Official Secrets Act and dutifully signed it.'

Olive's first billet was in Bedford where the woman

of the house was very unhappy at being forced to take a tenant and insisted Olive couldn't stay around the house during the evening.

'For the few months I was there she made my life miserable. I was turned out in the evenings as I was in the way.'

There was a large American barracks in Bedford and at night the town was full of American troops, so a woman on her own was the subject of constant unwanted attention.

'I was petrified. Later I made a friend in my section and we joined forces and went to another billet, again in Bedford, to a Mr and Mrs Buick, who had two children. They were completely and absolutely magnificent, never probed, always there for us.'

Olive was put to work in the section dealing with Japanese merchant ships. Her section was split into two, one half manned by civilian women and the other half by Wrens and Royal Navy officers.

'I found myself sitting at a table with six to eight Wrens. In the centre of the room was the boss, Major H.E. Martin. He was older than us, of course, and looked after his youngsters like a benevolent father. At the other end were three or four navy boys, all young and bright. I was quite happy, as I'd really wanted to join the Wrens.'

The codebreakers in Kilindini had broken the Japanese merchant navy code, which was made up of blocks of five figures each representing a Japanese term or syllable. So many messages were being sent by the Japanese merchant ships, known as '*Maru*', transporting troops and supplies around the Indian and Pacific Oceans that Kilindini had been able to recreate the entire codebook. Olive, the Wrens and the navy officers they worked with used this to decode the messages.

'We put the five-figure blocks, typed on flimsy paper, into clear English letters and constructed clear messages, such as: "*Otaru Maru* leaving Manila at 0200 hrs for Singapore arrives such and such." These messages were then passed to Major Martin. We didn't know what was happening in any other part of the section: the need-to-know syndrome was very much to the fore.'

Olive didn't get involved in the social life at Bletchley because her billet in Bedford was too far away, and being on shifts all the time didn't help.

'When I did get time off, I would remain in Bedford, sometimes with a Wren, whose name I have forgotten but who introduced me to Mozart. She would drag me into her favourite music shop, and we would land in the booths and listen to records. My recollection of hearing *Eine Kleine Nachtmusik* for the first time is still very vivid.'

The many odd characters Olive met at Bletchley made a very firm impression on her, like one clever young man who could only work if he had a bottle of whisky beside him. It was rumoured that the Foreign Office supplied him with a bottle a day until he had a breakdown and had to be taken away.

'I remember passing him in the corridors, always dressed in a pin-stripe suit, papers under his arm, muttering to himself, and a strong smell of malt wafting by with him. Another bright specimen divested himself of all his clothing and galloped round the lake with the army in hot pursuit, cheered on by us spectators on the banks, and the Wrens rowing lustily on the lake.'

In late 1943, with the Japanese retreating, the codebreakers in Kilindini began moving back to Colombo, a move that was to lead to tragedy. Eight Wren Typex operators en route from Kenya to Ceylon were killed in February 1944 when their ship, the *Khedive Ismail*, was sunk by a Japanese submarine.

With Italy now out of the war after surrendering in September 1943, more resources were thrown into the war against Japan and several hundred Wrens were trained at Bletchley Park before being posted to Colombo. Dorothy Robertson was a traffic analyst, studying the radio messages for hints of what the Japanese were planning to do. After several weeks of training, during which they lived in Woburn Abbey, Dorothy and sixty other Wrens were shipped out to Colombo.

'We must have had several submarine scares, as we often zigzagged en route, but life was so exciting with only some sixty Wrens and forty female army nurses on board and with five to six thousand servicemen. We really had a marvellous time.'

The troops' access to the women was 'rationed', with different batches allowed to chat to them at different times and dancing on deck with a new batch of men every night. Things started to hot up when they reached the Suez Canal.

'We began to notice a lot of landing craft moving towards us filled with men in white helmets. As they came alongside, one helmet looked upwards at us and emitted a loud cry: "Gee, dames!" Whereupon the whole flotilla of landing craft looked up and bawled: "Gee, dames!" Over the following days, the Yanks were also rationed to meet us, but somehow they seemed to appear here and there on our deck. They were often very amusing and terrible flirts. Our British lads were absolutely furious and used to surround us, four or five to one Wren, as an anti-Yank bodyguard.'

The Wrens were quartered in the grounds of Kent House, a large colonial house; whitewashed huts with thatched palm leaf roofs provided cabins for around five hundred Wrens. They worked at the HMS *Anderson* intercept site half an hour away in the middle of the jungle. There were around a thousand men to every girl on the island and there were always plenty of invitations to dances in the messes of the various units based in Ceylon.

'The favourite evening spot was the little nightclub, the Silver Fawn, where we'd be taken for a really glamorous evening's dinner-dancing, the live band playing favourite dance tunes, the lights low, flowers for one's dress, gorgeous food.

'You can imagine how spoiled we were, and we loved it. It was incredibly heady stuff for girls of our age. We were only in our early twenties, and there was usually the knowledge that the boyfriend would be leaving for India or Burma soon, perhaps never to return. How different and naive we were; one never heard of any misbehaviour. We had all been brought up so much more strictly then.'

*

Back at Bletchley, John Tiltman continued to lead the way
in breaking Japanese codes. He'd broken the Japanese
military attaché code in mid-1942 and the main Japanese
Air Force code in early 1943. By the time Mary Wisbey
arrived at Bletchley in late 1943, there were so many
Japanese sections in Block F that the long corridor
running through it was known as 'the Burma Road' after
the 700-mile-long British supply route from Burma into
southwest China. Mary was put into a sub-section of the
Japanese Air Section.

'The first job I had to do was extremely boring: the call-
sign index was terribly behind as no one had worked on
it for some time. I had to work so terribly hard to bring it
up to date. It took quite a long time as I was doing it on
my own.'

The rest of Mary's JappyWaaf soon arrived but were put
into separate departments and, although they were
all working on Japanese codes in Block F, and most were
working in different sub-sections of the Japanese Air
Section, none knew what any of the others were doing.
But they still socialised together. The JappyWaaf were virtually inseparable.

'In our spare time we'd hare off to London to get away
from Bletchley. All sorts of nice things like dancing and
theatres and entertainment and decent food. You had
to have an antidote to the work. I played a lot of tennis,
on the famous Bletchley tennis courts, and acted in the
Bletchley Park players.'

During one of the most popular plays they put on, Mary
took the lead role of Cecily Harrington in *Love from a*

Stranger, based on the Agatha Christie short story *Philomel Cottage*.

Betty Vine-Stevens worked on Japanese military codes. She and her sister hadn't gone to school; their mother, a music teacher, taught them at home in the small village of Richard's Castle, near Ludlow in Shropshire. Betty's mother had spent a year in Germany during the First World War, so the girls grew up speaking both English and German. In 1937, Betty was sent to Germany to spend three months with a family at Herrnhut, near Dresden.

'I attended school with the two daughters. We were obliged to stand to attention and give the Hitler salute at the beginning and end of every class. I didn't fully comprehend the German threat but felt it was diplomatic to join with the class requirement to salute. The girls' father did try to convey to me the local anxiety about the situation and the Hitler regime but my German wasn't good enough to understand what he was saying.'

Back in England, Betty went to a domestic science college near Shrewsbury but in the summer of 1941 she decided she was wasting her time learning how to cook sausage rolls and that she ought to be doing something to help King and country.

'Things were getting very hard on the war front and four of us decided we'd had enough of domestic science and all joined up. I went into the Auxiliary Territorial Service, which was the women's army, one went into the Wrens and the other two went into the WAAF.'

The first female equivalent of the Army, the Women's Army Auxiliary Corps, had been established during the

First World War but disbanded afterwards. As tension with Germany increased in the summer of 1938, a new women's army, the Auxiliary Territorial Service (ATS), was set up. The basic training was longer than for the other two women's services. New recruits had to do six weeks of marching, physical training and acclimatisation to service life. They were given equal military status with regular soldiers in 1941, but pay for Betty and the other ATS women was only two-thirds of that for the men, even when they were doing exactly the same job.

'We got ten shillings and sixpence during basic training but there were no deductions for rent or food and that took us quite a long way – we were able to go to the pictures and buy our own toiletries. We didn't want for anything. Basic training was a complete culture shock after a very sheltered life in the country. We had women instructors mostly but I remember one male instructor smacking me across the backside. I said: "How dare you?" And that was the end of that!'

At the end of her army training Betty was sent to Devonshire House in London's Piccadilly, where the Intelligence Corps recruited its personnel. She had an interview in what was fairly simple German and passed with flying colours. They didn't waste any time. She was given a rail warrant to Bletchley and sent off immediately. It was late by the time she got there and she and another ATS girl were taken straight to their billet. But they were forced to share a bed and next morning asked to be moved. Betty was eventually settled in a large house in Loughton, five miles northwest of Bletchley Park.

'I was very happy there. It was a lovely family in a very big house. There were five of them and three of us and it was very comfortable. They had a very big garden where they produced their own fruit and vegetables. So compared with what other people had to put up with as far as rations were concerned, we were extremely well fed.'

Betty was given a security lecture in the mansion by an Intelligence Corps captain who placed his gun on the desk in front of her while she read and signed the Official Secrets Act. Then she was taken upstairs and put to work in the Military Section, working on intercepted German police messages. Sometime around the end of 1943, she was moved to the Japanese Military Section in Block F where her job was to rewrite decoded messages so that it wasn't obvious they'd been produced by breaking the codes. They had to look as if they'd come from some other source like a human spy.

'One was given these messages and you had to put them into different wording so that it could be put out in this disguised form. Everything went out under a double-envelope system with different addresses. There were a lot of numbers on the outside one so that the dispatch rider could tell where it was supposed to go and then someone else opened it and sent it on to the address on the inside envelope. But as with everything we did, we knew very little of the next step.'

Although she was dealing with the actual messages, Betty was never aware of what impact any of them might have had on the war. The strict rules on not discuss-ing anything relating to what they were doing left her entirely in the dark as to how important her own role might be.

'But while small-fry like me didn't fully understand the importance of our own input, we did understand that it was imperative that we kept at it and that we did so in the utmost secrecy.'

No one was in any doubt about the importance of winning the war and even in the relative safety of Bletchley Park it sometimes impinged on their lives in a very distressing way. Not only did many of the women have boyfriends or husbands away at war, there was always the risk that close relatives living in the major cities might become victims of the German bombing. Mark Glover, an army sergeant working with Betty, became very worried when he couldn't get hold of his wife.

'He'd been telephoning or trying to telephone his wife without success. So he asked if he could have time off to go and see her and his son and make sure they were safe. I shall never forget that poor man coming back into the office and saying: "All I found was my boy's tie." His house had been destroyed by a doodlebug, with his wife and son inside.'

Mark's brother-in-law was the pianist Jack Byfield, who visited Bletchley to give a recital, one of a number of prominent musicians who performed in the assembly hall. Betty's mother had instilled a love of music in her daughters and Betty was a member of several music sections.

'Social life at Bletchley was very good. We had the Bach choir under Herbert Murrill, which I had the audacity to join, a gramophone group and the Madrigal Society.

That was always good fun, sometimes singing outdoors, sometimes indoors, and of course once the camp was built we had darts and table tennis. The plays were put on once every three months and were always extremely good and there was an orchestra run by David Warwick. Despite the sometimes boring duties, the atmosphere was happy and relaxed, with the usual services humour. We worked hard and we played hard.'

Once the Shenley Road camp was built, Betty had to move out of her billet into one of the newly constructed wooden huts. They had bitumen floors, which camp commandant Colonel George Fillingham, irritated by his lack of control over the young ATS women who lived in *his* camp, insisted they tried to polish.

'The huts we slept in were thrown up in a great hurry and had thin walls so in the winter one's flannel would be frozen by the morning. They were very, very basic conditions, but we were young, we didn't mind. I was a sergeant by then. We had our own mess. It was typical army rations, dried egg, a certain amount of vegetables, I don't remember very much meat. It was a case of survival, really, and you just accepted what was put in front of you.'

Once Mary had got the call-sign index up to date, she was moved on to tracking the Japanese Army Air Force's 'order of battle', where each unit was based and how it fitted into the overall structure.

'Our tools were fairly basic. Paper and pencil. That was our equipment. There were no windows in the blocks. We had huge maps on the walls with pins and flags for our order-of-battle work. There were just thin glass ventilators high up near the ceiling.'

On one particularly hot day, Mary decided to open the ventilators. She stood on the desk and looked out through the glass at a stud farm on the other side of the perimeter fence.

'I saw for the first time these wonderful horses in the field next to the block and, having got up there, realised there was a nice shelf which I decided to use for my pending tray. The summer was very hot so I opened the ventilator and thought nothing of it.'

A couple of days later, a security officer came into her office clutching some very dirty-looking pieces of paper. They were from Mary's pending tray and had blown out of the ventilator and into the field.

'He told me that I must never leave traffic by an open window or ventilator and I said I was very sorry. He gave the sheets back to me – they stunk of manure. The horses had done their worst. They obviously didn't like what they'd read.'

Most of the sections dealing with Japanese Army material were staffed by a mixture of ATS, Intelligence Corps and Foreign Office civilians, and most did even more repetitive work than that done by Betty or Mary. Gladys Sweetland was sent to the mysterious 'Station X' as a young ATS corporal after being selected at an anonymous set of offices in Praed Street near London's Paddington Station.

'We were there for several days being interviewed by lots of different people, most of them officers. Then finally we were told we were being transferred to Bletchley. It was really rather weird.'

Once she arrived at the Park, Gladys was sat down in a hut and told to copy out a series of messages in different-coloured inks underneath each other on large sheets of graph paper.

'I know it sounds ridiculous but we never asked what they did with the sheets of messages. It was all so secret. Even with the other girls in the ATS we only ever asked: "Where do you work?" And they'd say: "Oh, Hut 6" or "Block F" or whatever. We never asked each other what we actually did.'

The first woman Gladys was billeted with had two young children and wanted her to stay in and look after them all the time so she could go out. Fortunately, Gladys was moved to a much nicer woman's house.

'She was middle-aged. She had a son in the RAF and her attitude was that if she could treat people billeted with her kindly, then perhaps other people would treat her son the same way. She would insist on bringing me breakfast in bed after I'd worked the late shift.'

The work might be unrewarding, other than in the knowledge that it must in some way be helping the war effort, but as with many of the young women from working-class backgrounds, Gladys was introduced to a world she would never have otherwise known.

'Bletchley Park was a wonderful location and sometimes we just sat in the grounds in fine weather for our break. There was a whole group of us who used to go around together to pubs and concerts.'

Gladys acquired a lifelong love of opera and ballet after seeing both for the first time in the assembly hall just outside the gates when the D'Oyly Carte Opera Company and the Ballet Rambert performed for the codebreakers. She also took part in the Bletchley Park Recreational Club gramophone section, discussing the merits of various pieces of music she would never have heard had she not been sent to Bletchley Park.

'I shall never forget the comradeship and meeting all those different types of people who were there. I never thought, leaving school at fourteen and a half, that I would be able to have a proper conversation with a university professor.'

By now the breaking of the Japanese codes was being done at so many locations – in India, Ceylon, Washington, Australia, Hawaii and on the front line in Burma and across the Pacific islands – that it was impossible for the codebreakers at Bletchley to know which piece of intelligence was produced where. So there was very little of the satisfaction that those working on the German codes had from their successes.

But one series of messages sent by the Japanese and broken at Bletchley was to be vitally important to the preparations for D-Day and the Allied invasion of Europe, almost as important as Dilly Knox's break into the 'Spy Enigma'. In October 1943, Oshima Hiroshi, the Japanese ambassador in Berlin, toured the German fortifications along the French coast, the so-called Atlantic Wall. The Germans showed him everything and briefed him on their plans to repel the Allied invasion, which they expected to come around the northeastern French port of Calais.

Oshima sent back a detailed report of everything he had learned to Tokyo. The British were able to intercept the report, which was sent using the international commercial teleprinter circuits, and the Japanese Diplomatic Section, based in Elmer's School on the south-western edge of Bletchley Park, used the Purple machine supplied by the Americans to decode it.

The Japanese ambassador had provided a detailed rundown of German forces in both France and Belgium, listing the number of divisions, where they were based and how they were controlled. He also listed the reinforcements that would take place in the event of an Allied invasion, which included three top SS armoured divisions. Oshima provided the first authoritative figure for the number of German forces in France, which he put at 1.4 million, and confirmed that the Germans believed the Allied forces would come ashore around Calais. That knowledge would be absolutely vital to the D-Day deception plan that the British were putting together to confuse the Germans over where the invasion would take place.

The gaps in Oshima's report – and there seemed at the time to be very few – were more than filled in by Colonel Ito Seiichi, the Japanese military attaché in Berlin, who made his own tour of the entire German coastal defences, sending a highly detailed 32-part report back to Tokyo. This was encoded using the Japanese military attaché code that had been broken by John Tiltman, and was decoded in Block F. Colonel Ito gave a comprehensive description of every part of the fortifications, detailing everything from the heaviest artillery battery to the smallest collection of flame-throwers.

The RAF had been flying aerial reconnaissance operations along the French and Belgian coastline for several years, taking photographs of every inch of the Atlantic Wall, but the intelligence provided by Bletchley was far more comprehensive and allowed intelligence chiefs to send the RAF aircraft back so that more photographs could be taken of areas highlighted in the two reports.

The codebreakers expected the Japanese naval attaché in Berlin, Rear Admiral Kojima Hideo, to make his own tour of the defences as well, but they were struggling to break the Coral machine cipher he used for his reports to Tokyo. A joint British-American operation to try to unravel the system was under way using methods pioneered by Hut 8 in the breaking of the German naval Enigma, but they were struggling to make any progress. In February 1944, Hugh Alexander flew to Washington to lead the attack there and Joan Clarke and other members of Hut 8 stepped up their efforts at Bletchley. Finally, in March, they cracked it.

Just a few weeks later, the Japanese naval attaché went ahead with his inspection of the German defences and his report back to Tokyo was decoded at Bletchley. It was more authoritative than Oshima's and critically – given that D-Day was only a couple of weeks away – Admiral Kojima was briefed by General Erwin Rommel, who was now commanding the German forces defending the French coast, on how he planned to respond to an Allied invasion. Rommel made it clear that he intended 'to destroy the enemy near the coast, most of all on the beaches, without allowing them to penetrate any considerable distance inland'.

The Allies were just a couple of weeks away from D-Day and – thanks to the codebreakers – they knew where the Germans thought they would attack, they knew the Germans believed the Double Cross deception plan, they knew every detail of the German defences, they even knew precisely how the Germans intended to respond to the invasion. Everything they did could be tailored to make maximum use of this information to catch the Germans on the wrong foot. It was to prove vital to the success of the D-Day invasion.

Marion Graham was recruited to work on the Japanese codes in early 1944. She'd been born in Bombay where her grandfather had been one of the engineers who built the Great Indian Peninsula Railway. Her father worked for the railway and Marion was sent home when she was five to live with her aunt in Breconshire. She was fifteen when war began and after leaving school she helped with refugees while waiting to go to secretarial college.

'It was called Mrs Hester's Secretarial College. It was quite famous. They'd been going for years and they always got you top jobs. The college had been evacuated from London to Lincolnshire.'

After completing the course, Marion took a job while she was waiting to be called up. She'd volunteered for the Wrens so was rather surprised when she was summoned to the Foreign Office, which unbeknown to her was in touch with Mrs Hester's looking for likely recruits for Bletchley.

'Bletchley couldn't just recruit from the Labour Exchange, of course, so at first they had to recruit the director's friends, get admirals' daughters, generals' daughters and suchlike, but then the net had to be spread wider and the Foreign Office was in touch with the secretarial colleges.'

There were a number of old 'Hester's Girls' at Bletchley, including two of Marion's best friends from the college, the Glassborow twins, Valerie and Mary.[1] Initially, Marion was in a terraced house in Stony Stratford with a working-class family. It was not at all what she was used to. The lavatory was down the end of a very narrow back garden.

'But they were a good family. The house was spotlessly clean. You could skid on the lino. Outside loo. No bathroom. It was simple. But they were a very decent family. Then they had family troubles and I had to move to Bedford, which I didn't really like because it was such a long way. But the people there were a very nice family too so I was very fortunate with my billets.'

Marion started out working in Block F typing up Japanese messages that were being sent to Washington and Colombo, mostly about Japanese troop movements. Around the end of 1944, she was moved to a unit called Clinical Monitoring of Y, or CMY, based in the old Hut 6, where her job was reading the intercepted Japanese messages to make sure that the intercept stations, which were also known as the 'Y' Stations, were taking

---

[1] Valerie Glassborow was the paternal grandmother of HRH Catherine, Duchess of Cambridge.

all the messages from the various networks they were monitoring. Different stations on the Japanese networks frequently transmitted on different frequencies so an operator at an intercept station monitoring a specific frequency would only hear what one of the stations said. The responses were on a different frequency again and it was important that the operators found both frequencies so the intelligence analysts and reporters could see everything that was being said.

'Reams of paper used to come in and then you had to check it all off. It was incredibly tedious but there were a jolly nice lot of girls there. We just made the best of it, and the Glassborow twins were on the same shift as me, which was good because they were fun.'

The Allies were by now aware that a sizeable faction within the Japanese government would be prepared to sue for peace, but the messages being decoded at Bletchley showed that, despite horrific losses, the Japanese military remained determined to fight on.

The only man capable of bringing the Japanese Army to heel was the Emperor himself. On 12 July 1945, the Allies intercepted a Purple message from Tokyo to Japan's ambassador in Moscow ordering him to hand the Russians an urgent plea for peace from Emperor Hirohito. The message was sent just days before the Potsdam Conference at which Soviet leader Joseph Stalin was to meet with Winston Churchill and Harry Truman, the new US President.

Truman was already on his way to Potsdam when Hirohito's peace approach was decoded. Allied intelligence had advised that if the Emperor ordered the Japanese armed forces to surrender they would obey but that if 'unconditional surrender' meant the Emperor must lose his throne and be treated as a war criminal, the Japanese would fight to the last man.

Four days after Emperor Hirohito's message was intercepted, the first atomic bomb was tested in the New Mexico desert. For reasons which remain inexplicable, and despite an acceptance by both America and Britain that the Emperor would have to be retained in order to control post-war Japan, no attempt was made privately to reassure the Japanese that he would not be forced to stand down. America and Britain issued an ultimatum to Japan. If there was not an immediate and unconditional surrender, it would lead to 'the utter devastation of the Japanese homeland'.

Lacking any assurances over the future of the Emperor, the Japanese were never likely to surrender. At 8.15 local time on the morning of 6 August 1945, a United States B29 bomber dropped an atomic bomb on the southwestern Japanese port of Hiroshima, flattening two-thirds of the city. Three days later, a second bomb exploded over the port of Nagasaki, razing it to the ground. More than 200,000 people died as a direct result, with the number of deaths from the long-term effects of radiation impossible to calculate.

Even before the news that the atomic bomb had been dropped on Hiroshima was officially announced, the messages arriving in Bletchley Park provided Rosemary Calder with a terrifying vision of what had taken place.

'I was on a day watch by myself and all this stuff came in and it was total gibberish. I didn't know the bomb had been dropped but you could tell from the disruption of all the messages that something terrible had happened. You could just feel the people standing there screaming their heads off.'

The dropping of the atomic bombs led the Japanese to sue for peace. Only then were they told that – despite the insistence on 'unconditional surrender' – the Emperor was always going to be allowed to keep his throne. Had they been told that two weeks earlier, the war would almost certainly have been ended without recourse to the atomic bomb, and the countless loss of life.

Marion Graham and the Glassborow twins were on duty in the Clinical Monitoring Section on the morning of 15 August 1945 when their boss Commander Williams came in and said: 'Well done, girls. A signal's been intercepted and it does appear that the Japanese are about to surrender.'

Marion and the rest of them just sat there not sure what to say. Commander Williams shuffled about a bit looking embarrassed, as if he wasn't sure what to do next. Then he said: 'Well, you bloody well get on with your work now,' before adding that he would come back if he heard anything more. Marion and her friends didn't have long to wait.

'About half an hour later, he came back and said: "The war's over." It was quite a moment. Of course, I wasn't the first but I must have been one of the first to know and he did say that a message had gone to the King and to the Prime Minister, so it was tremendously exciting.'

The girls didn't have anything else to do so they just got on with their work, pointless though it now seemed, and when they went home on the transport they didn't say anything to anyone about it, unsure whether it was all still secret. When Marion got back to her billet one of the family asked her if she'd heard the news. The war was over.

'I couldn't say, "Yes, I know," so I just said: "How wonderful." And that was it.'

10

An Extraordinary Army of People

Sally Norton was working the night shift in the Admiralty Citadel on Horse Guards Parade when the news came through from Bletchley that Germany had surrendered. It made for a very busy night and she still hadn't managed to collect her thoughts when she left work that morning and headed home to her flat.

'I was too tired to be deliriously happy and just felt a deep contentment, but as I walked along the Mall the sound of church bells began to peal out all over London. We had not heard those bells for five and a half years. I went back to my flat and fell asleep, too tired to take my clothes off.'

That evening, at a party to celebrate victory in Europe, Sally met her future husband Bill Astor, a Conservative politician and the future 3rd Viscount Astor. Afterwards she joined the throngs of people celebrating in Trafalgar Square and along the capital's streets. She'd had a wonderfully rewarding job but it was coming to an end and she wasn't sure that anything she did would ever be quite so exciting again.

'Looking back to VE Day, reliving the happiness and relief that the conflict was over, I remember a feeling of being forgotten. No campaign ribbons. Not that we deserved any. No certificate such as our colleagues in the Red Cross received. Just nothing. Even a pat on the back might have elevated the psyche, but if you work for Special Intelligence that's what you must expect and on reflection it was well worth it.

'We formed great bonds with the people we worked with. There was an extraordinary army of people there from all walks of life. Wrens, girls like me, people in uniform, army, navy, air force, Americans. All walks of life, all classes of life, especially among the Wrens. Literally walk down any street in London, you'd see the same mix of people.'

Sally and Bill Astor had one son, William, later the 4th Viscount Astor, but were divorced in 1953 and she then married Thomas Baring. They had one adopted son, Edward, and were divorced in 1965. Sally never remarried. She died in 2013, a couple of weeks after her ninety-third birthday.

Colette St George-Yorke and some of her fellow Bombe operators were standing on the balcony at the small 'Wrennery' in Steeple Claydon when the bells on the little village church of St Michael started ringing. They didn't stop.

'Someone came up and said the war's over. We just stood there in the window and cried.'

The next day they were sent back to Stanmore to dismantle the Bombes. Roma Davies, or Wren Stenning as she then was, was at Eastcote, also dismantling the Bombes. Nothing was to remain of them, supposedly on Mr Churchill's orders. It was imperative that no one found out they'd been breaking the Enigma codes. Whether the decision to destroy the Bombes was made by the Prime Minister is a moot point, but Roma and the other Wrens undoubtedly believed it was.

'We were always told Mr Churchill was the only one to know our secret; so naturally it was very easy to believe that he ordered the dismantling of the machines. I was one of the people who helped to take them to bits, right down to very tiny bits. We had huge bonfires to destroy all the paperwork. We demolished every bit of evidence of our ever being there.'

Roma was then sent to Bletchley to work on the Japanese codes until the war in the Far East came to an end. Dorothy Robertson was still out in Colombo when Japan surrendered. She found herself doing what would be the most moving and at the same time most satisfying job of her life. Thousands of prisoners of war released from camps across the Far East were being brought back to Britain, stopping off in Colombo for a period of rehabilitation.

'Three of us sorted mail for incoming ex-PoWs and helped any who wanted to send a message home. It was hard to remain dry-eyed when a lad would open and read the first letter he had had from home for several years, from a mother, wife or sweetheart. One chap read out to me: "She says, I am still waiting," as he broke down and wept.'

They weren't all members of the forces. Expatriate Britons, many of them women, had been swept up by the Japanese and subjected to appalling brutality in the camps. The women were taken to a 'beauty parlour' set up by the Wrens, where they could take a shower, have their hair cut and styled, and make-up put on their faces for the first time in four or five years.

'It was good for their morale but to see their worn and gaunt skin underneath was sad. We were all very moved and felt immensely humble in the presence of the PoWs who had suffered so much and for so long.'

Finally Dorothy was sent home on a troopship, much more crowded and far less exciting than the one she'd gone out on. Britain was effectively bankrupt, beholden to the United States for the cash needed to keep the country going, with every penny having to be watched.

'Life afterwards in post-war Britain was really grey and cheerless. There were innumerable shortages, and ration cards and clothing coupons were to continue for some time yet. People had gone through a ghastly time, but the knowledge that we – incredibly – had won this six-year war, when at times it seemed impossible, was everything.'

The Government Code and Cypher School moved to the Eastcote site under its new name of the Government Communications Headquarters, or GCHQ. Most of the temporary Foreign Office staff recruited during the war were being laid off. Pre-war staff like Barbara Abernethy and Phoebe Senyard were told they could keep their jobs, but others were being made redundant with just one week's wages. Barbara was left to close up the Park.

'The General Post Office was going to take the place over. So we just left everything as it was. We closed down the huts, put all the files away and sent them down to Eastcote. I was the last person left at Bletchley Park. I locked the gates and then took the key down to Eastcote. That was it.'

It was an emotional departure for Barbara. That midnight meeting between Commander Denniston and the Americans had changed her life. Barbara fell in love with one of the US naval officers sent to Bletchley as a liaison officer. Joe Eachus already had a wife back in America, but he was soon to be divorced and, in 1947, Barbara was transferred to the GCHQ liaison office in the United States, where she and Joe were married. After leaving GCHQ in 1956, she worked at the British Consulate in Boston and became a vice-consul in charge of media liaison. Barbara was appointed MBE as a result of her work in the consulate rather than for her work at Bletchley, and retired from the Consular Service in 1986. Joe had two sons from his previous marriage but Barbara and Joe never had any children of their own. Joe died in 2003 and Barbara in 2012.

Betty Vine-Stevens and Julie Lydekker flew to America at the end of the European war and spent the next few months working with the Americans on Japanese codes, enjoying the complete contrast to the depressing austerity of wartime Britain. They had every weekend off and enjoyed a variety of foods they'd never seen before, including inch-thick fillet steaks and real ice cream.

At the end of the war against Japan, they returned to Britain and were demobbed. Betty took a secretarial course 'for young gentlewomen' in London and then went home to Richard's Castle near Ludlow, but found it very difficult to get a job.

'I tried, of course, but you'd go to a prospective employer and they'd ask what you were doing during the war and you'd say you couldn't tell them. I just said I was not at liberty to say. Faces went blank. They didn't understand and they were quite shirty.'

Then she applied for a job as secretary to the headmaster at Ludlow Grammar School. When he interviewed her they both realised that they had seen each other at Bletchley, so she didn't have to explain, and she got the job, although neither of them ever said anything about their work in the war.

'That was before the veil of secrecy was lifted. We didn't say anything about it. We just knew that we'd both been there. But we didn't ever talk about it.'

Betty later joined the Territorial Army and worked as an administrative officer for a number of years before getting married in 1970 at the age of forty-seven; sadly, her husband Alfred died seven years later. Bletchley remains very close to her heart and she now gives talks about the work there.

'It has not always been easy to talk about it but once you are able to talk about something like that it all comes gushing out. It was a very important thing. I feel very much that I've been privileged to be involved in it.'

*

As one of the pre-war staff of the Government Code and Cypher School, Phoebe Senyard moved to Eastcote with Barbara Abernethy, travelling into work from Peckham each day on the Tube. Both Phoebe's mother and her brother Henry survived the war. Phoebe retired in August 1951, with GCHQ then in the process of transferring to Cheltenham. She, her mother and Henry moved to Croydon, where she settled down in retirement with many happy memories of her time at Bletchley Park.

'They were happy days. The people that I knew in the German Naval Section were a very kind, cooperative crowd; nothing was too much trouble for them to do and I could never wish to work with finer people. They were a grand crowd.'

Phoebe's mother died a year after they moved to Croydon. Phoebe herself died in 1983, aged ninety-one. She never married.

Mavis Batey (née Lever), Joan Clarke and Margaret Rock all went to Eastcote with GCHQ to work on Russian codes. Margaret was appointed MBE at the end of the war and continued working at GCHQ until her retirement in 1963. She never married and died in 1983 at the age of eighty, having never spoken about anything she did either at Bletchley or for GCHQ. Joan Clarke was appointed MBE in 1947 and continued to work for GCHQ until 1952 when she married Jock Murray, one of her colleagues at Cheltenham. She rejoined GCHQ in 1962 and retired in 1977. She had no children and died in 1996, aged seventy-nine.

Mavis left GCHQ in 1947 to start a family and when Keith was appointed to a post at the High Commission in Ottawa she went with him. They had two daughters and a son, and Mavis stayed at home to bring them up. Then in the 1960s, Keith became 'Secretary of the Chest' at Oxford University, the chief financial officer of the university. The Bateys lived in a house in the grounds of the university-owned Nuneham Courtenay estate and Mavis began work on the restoration of the eighteenth-century gardens. It led to a pioneering role in garden history that she said was heavily influenced by her former boss Dilly Knox.

'Working for an eccentric genius, whose motto was "Nothing is impossible", during the most formative years of my life made a lasting impression.'

The post-war period of the 1950s and 1960s were times of great change in Britain, much of it positive but a lot of it detrimental. The slogan 'new lives, new landscapes' was current and historic parks and estates were being destroyed by the construction of new roads. Mavis always insisted that it was Dilly's insistence that 'nothing is impossible' and the way that women were treated equally at Bletchley – in all aspects apart from pay – which gave her the confidence she needed for the fight to protect historic gardens and parks.

'Women who worked at Bletchley Park have much to be grateful for. It was a remarkable community where neither rank nor status counted and a girl of nineteen with a bright idea would be encouraged to take it forward, long before any official equality for women. Throughout Bletchley Park and its outstations all that mattered was getting the job done.'

Mavis was appointed MBE for her work on protecting historic gardens, having received no honours for her many achievements at Bletchley. She wrote many books on garden history including *Jane Austen and the English Landscape* and *Alexander Pope: The Poet and the Landscape*, and also an affectionate and much-needed biography of her old boss, *Dilly: The Man Who Broke Enigmas*. Keith died in 2010 and Mavis in 2013.

When Jane Hughes left Bletchley she took up a scholarship at the Royal Academy of Music and trained as a professional singer, marrying her Royal Navy officer fiancé Ted Fawcett and having her two children while she was studying.

'I went to my final exam with one of my children inside me and the other one asleep in a carrycot and the examiners kept asking me if I wanted to sit down because I was seven months pregnant.'

Jane spent fifteen years as a professional singer, performing a lot of opera and recital work of which the most prominent roles were Scylla in *Scylla et Glaucus*, as the Sorceress in *Dido and Aeneas* and singing '*Seit ich ihn gesehen*' ('Since I Saw Him') from Schumann's song cycle *Frauenliebe und -leben* Opus 42 (*A Woman's Love and Life*).

It was 'a very exciting time' in her life but it meant touring and too much time spent away from her children, so in 1963 she gave up professional singing and took a job as the secretary of the Victorian Society, set up five years earlier to prevent the demolition of old Victorian buildings and their replacement with the characterless concrete and glass popular in the 1950s, 60s and 70s.

Despite Jane becoming what was effectively the chief administrator, it was not a lucrative position as the society had little money. When Sir Nikolaus Pevsner, the society's director, wrote offering her the post, he said he was glad to tell her that 'the ill-paid job for the *enthusiast* has gone to you'.

Working from home on her own portable typewriter, Jane joined Pevsner in a whirlwind campaign to prevent the destruction of the country's great Victorian buildings. It was a remarkable pairing. The biggest battle was with British Rail, whose executives had just sparked a public outcry by knocking down the main arch in front of Euston Station when Jane appeared on the scene. They now found themselves frustrated at every turn by the woman they took to calling 'The Furious Mrs Fawcett'.

The most dramatic victory came in 1967, when with the assistance of Prince Philip and John Betjeman the society succeeded in ensuring the listing of the St Pancras locomotive shed and the station's Midland Grand Hotel, both of which British Rail had been determined to knock down. It was a campaign of which Jane was very proud.

'The fact that St Pancras is intact is one of my special achievements. Not only the train shed but the hotel. I never thought it would be a hotel again. But it is. It's quite remarkable and it retains so many original features. It is a magnificent building by any standards.'

Jane stepped down in 1976 and was appointed MBE for her services to conservation as well as being elected an honorary fellow of the Royal Institute of British Architects. As with Mavis Batey, a close friend of both Jane and her husband, the refusal to give up engrained at Bletchley had served her well in her post-war careers.

'It was a very exciting period. They were exhausting days because we always seemed to be in a minority. It was a big undertaking to turn over a whole nation from one attitude towards architecture to another.'

Marigold Philips stayed in the Wrens for a while after leaving Bletchley. She was sent to a base in Cornwall to teach sailors about Shakespeare, which was supposed to help them adapt back to civilian life.

'It was tremendous fun but totally pointless. All they did was look at my black-stocking-clad legs as I stood on the platform.'

The majority of young Wrens simply wanted to get back to their ordinary lives, and for most that meant finding a husband and settling down with a young family. Despite her previous determination to get herself a university education, Marigold was no different.

'All we wanted was "normality"; to have, in this order, a husband, a baby, a house and a car. I had no ambitions and I think that was very common. It had seemed so unnatural, the life we had led, that we swung too far the other way and of course a great many people bitterly regretted it.'

The marriages that took place during the war or in its immediate aftermath frequently fell apart. Marigold was lucky. She married David, an army officer, and because he was posted to a succession of overseas bases, she had the opportunity to work as a teacher in schools for servicemen's children, so she had a rewarding job. Most were not so fortunate.

'We all heard stories of the young mothers with good brains who suddenly found they had a husband at work all day and two small children at home and went nearly batty with frustration. It was a quite severe social problem after the war.'

Marigold and David had two sons and a daughter but eventually the marriage crumbled and she married another army officer, Warren Freeman-Attwood. She didn't tell either of her husbands what she'd done in the war and when the news emerged in 1974, when the former head of the MI6 Air Section Frederick Winterbotham published *The Ultra Secret*, she was shocked. Neither she nor any of her friends who had worked with her were happy that the story they were told must never be revealed was now the subject of a bestselling book by one of the senior officers in charge of keeping it secret.

'It was horrible. We hated it. We didn't like the secret coming out. It was like having a bit of skin that had grown over something peeled off. The secrecy was so engrained that even now talking about it still feels like you're gossiping to someone. I still hate talking about it.'

But like the vast majority of the thousands of women who worked at Bletchley, Marigold regards her small part with great pride. At the end of the war, 10,471 people worked at Bletchley Park, 7,000 of them women.

'It was hugely important for me, and I think it must have been for everybody who was there. Whether you liked it or not you were one of the geese who laid the golden eggs and in your lowest moment, when you're feeling like shit, at least you can say: "I played my part. I did my bit to help win the war."'

Most of the Bletchley veterans were determined to keep the secret until they died. They'd been indoctrinated into staying quiet forever, so the Winterbotham revelations were a great shock. Joy Higgins met her first husband Hugh at Bletchley. He worked in the Naval Section in Hut 4. Even though both of them had worked at Bletchley Park, Joy never told him what she did and he never told her what he'd done.

'People without our common background at Bletchley found it much more difficult to accept a partner's refusal to discuss the work there. It must have been hard for them.'

Hugh died in 1967, nine years before the government's decision to allow former codebreakers to tell their relatives what they did in the war, so even now Joy has only the vaguest idea of what her husband did; but she knows that, like her, he loved working at Bletchley.

'Nothing would ever compare with it. It had been a wonderful place to work: a classless society where brains, application and enthusiasm were the criteria. The ethos of Bletchley meant that women were treated as equals – years ahead of any "politically correct" diktats; that new schemes for tackling a job were never snubbed; it meant new ideas and not accepting old standards without question; it meant informality; it meant talking the same language with like-minded people, whether it was serious discussion or witty repartee.'

But for many years afterwards their work at Bletchley Park conditioned their lives. Joy felt for her husband, whose pre-war contemporaries had returned full of stories of bravery in the face of danger, of battles with the Germans or the Japanese. They had medals to prove that they had done their bit.

'They hadn't much respect for civilians who'd spent the war years as civil servants in the Foreign Office, not on active service. Things were not made easier by our reluctance to say anything at all. People were quick to label our evasions as rudeness.'

Maggie Broughton-Thompson had stayed in the Wrens after the war, becoming an officer and only leaving in 1952 when she married a naval officer. She never told him about Bletchley Park and was horrified one day to see a television documentary telling the story of how they broke the codes.

'I was sitting at home and my husband was watching a programme. I happened to glance up and at that precise moment there was a picture of the mansion and they were talking about it and I was so absolutely horrified. It was such a shock, I was jolly nearly sick.

'I sat there pointing at the television shouting, "No, No, No." He thought I'd gone mad, I think. It really was the most awful shock. We really were staying quiet for life. We were prepared to stay silent until our dying day.'

Mary Wisbey found herself caught in a tug-of-war after Japan surrendered. She was posted to London to work in air intelligence but Joe Hooper insisted on her returning to work for him in the Russian Air Section at Eastcote.

'I didn't want to go back. I wanted to stay in air intelligence. It was much more interesting work. I wanted to broaden my view.'

Eventually, she got herself posted to an air intelligence job in the RAF's Middle East headquarters in Egypt and after two years was offered the choice of a permanent commission in the WAAF or a job in MI6. She chose MI6 and worked for them in Germany and the Middle East. It's a period that even more than fifty years later she cannot discuss. Mary married John Every, a former RAF officer, in 1971 and they had fifteen very happy years together before he died. She'd kept in touch with all the other members of the JappyWaaf – Eileen, Evelyn, Cicely, Denise, Margaret and Peggy – and from the 1980s onwards they held annual reunions. They were so close that every time they met up it was as if they had only just seen each other the previous day in the Bletchley canteen.

'On the fiftieth anniversary of the day we met on the Japanese course we had a weekend in Stratford-on-Avon and celebrated fifty years of friendship during which time we'd never had the slightest quarrel or any kind of difficulty.'

They'd also been taken aback when the truth about Bletchley Park emerged in 1974 and it was not until that anniversary weekend at Stratford-on-Avon in 1992 that any of them talked about what they'd done during the war.

'That was the first time we discussed it, because at Bletchley Park none of us ever worked in the same office

so I never knew until then what anybody else did. I had
no idea. It is very difficult for people who didn't work at
Bletchley to realise what pressure we were under because
we had to bottle it all up. It affected the rest of our lives. I
never did tell my husband what I did during the war and
my parents also never knew what I did.'

Mair Thomas went back to the valleys to marry her
childhood sweetheart Russ, a conscientious objector who
had spent the war training to be a Baptist minister. She
died in 2013, but not before penning a beautiful memoir
of her time at Bletchley with her son Gethin Russell-
Jones, in which she spoke of how proud she was of her
war work.

'I had the most wonderful time in Bletchley. From
the first time I went into Hut 6 I felt special; privileged
to be there. There were plenty of things I found difficult
and hard at the time, but that's life anyway. To think
that I rubbed shoulders with some of the most brilliant
men that Britain has ever produced and played a part in
cracking the Enigma code is a source of daily amazement.
To this day, I'm not sure how a girl from a quiet Welsh
valley ended up in the centre of the action, but I am so
thankful that it happened. Despite the shift pattern and
the exhaustion and disorientation, there was exhilaration
to it all. I remember someone saying to me that we were
on the intellectual front line.'

Susan Wenham never married and only rarely discussed
her work in Hut 6 breaking the Enigma codes, but right
up until her death in 2009 at the age of ninety-seven, she

recalled 'the mixture of nuttiness, angst, hard slog, and euphoria' at Bletchley.

'Little things return to mind, the identical twins, wide cheeks and hair piled high and with an "important" folder of documents tucked under the arm, who were deputed to instruct newcomers about Enigma – although I felt they didn't understand it much better than I did.'

She remembered John Monroe, a 'brilliant' barrister and codebreaker who was deeply upset that 'with all that knowledge in his head' he was not allowed to fight alongside his contemporaries on the front line, and John Manisty, head of maths at Winchester, who had a fascination with trains and an encyclopedic knowledge of Bradshaw's, the national railways timetable, freely advising all and sundry on which trains they should take to get home as quickly as possible. He once told Susan how to get her horse back to Surrey without suffering any jolting stops that might lead to injuries.

'Among the Blisters I remember a lively half-French woman called Yvette, Mary Penney, who longed to get back to her career as a violinist, and a jolly, bouncy girl who relished bawdy jokes and left to become a nun. After the war it was bliss to go to bed every night at a sensible time and gradually lose the tiredness which had become a part of me, but it was many years before I lost the recurrent dream of a message with a strange frequency which I couldn't recognise.'

For many of the women who worked at Bletchley Park or on the Bombes the most distressing thing was never being able to tell their parents, to give them a sense that their daughter was doing something worthwhile, to make them proud of what they had achieved.

Olive Humble was on leave when Japan surrendered and when she got back to Bletchley she was given a week's pay, told she was no longer required and hauled back up before Commander Thatcher to be warned that if she ever said anything she would face thirty years in jail or the firing squad.

'I said farewell to the navy and to Major Martin, who gave me a glowing reference, including words like "National Importance". The Foreign Office one was even better: "Employed on important and highly specialised work of a secret nature. The Official Secrets Act precludes any information in connection with these duties." Heady stuff! Even better than navy cocoa.'

Olive immigrated to South Africa in 1947 with Doris Ward, one of her colleagues in the Japanese Naval Section, although neither of them knew what work the other had done at Bletchley. Olive married a couple of years later and had three children, seven grandchildren and six great-grandchildren. For many years her daughters thought she must have been a spy during the war. Olive eventually persuaded them otherwise but she and they still remain extremely proud of what she did at Bletchley.

'One didn't really realise what one was doing until afterwards, but we worked hard and we did help win the war. I know I was only a small cog but I remain tremendously proud of what we did.

'There is one thing I regret deeply. I was an only child, and on my first day home my father at dinner said, "What do you do at the Foreign Office?" I replied, "I cannot tell you. Sorry. Please don't ask me again." And he didn't; nor did my mother at any time. She died in the early 1960s and he in 1976, before I realised the silence had been lifted. I think they would have been so very proud.'

Christine Brooke-Rose went to Germany in the immediate aftermath of the war to carry out assessments of how successful the Allied bombing had been. On her return, she achieved her wartime ambition of going to university, reading English at Somerville College, Oxford. The feeling she had when she first arrived at Bletchley that she was somehow not up to the intellectual standard of those around her in Hut 3, never shared by her colleagues, drove her on to great intellectual heights. She married the Polish poet and novelist Jerzy Pietrkiewicz and obtained a doctorate in medieval literature at University College, London, before becoming an award-winning novelist and Professor of English Language and Literature at the University of Paris. One of her many highly praised experimental novels, *Remake*, was autobiographical and recorded her life at Bletchley, including the affair with Telford Taylor, with whom she remained friends right up to his death in 1998. Christine married three times but had no children and died in 2012 aged eighty-nine.

At the end of the war, Marion Graham and the Glassborow sisters were sent to GCHQ's Berkeley Street offices in London's West End to work on diplomatic codes. They lived in a hostel in Eaton Place and had plenty of time to attend the theatre or go to parties. They were told their temporary contracts were ending in April 1946, and Marion went to work for the British Council, promoting British culture abroad. She studied for a while in Perugia in Italy and then worked in Geneva for a year.

'I found it was quite difficult to settle in London after all that but eventually I got a job as a secretary to John Hall, the Conservative MP for Wycombe, and spent eight years working in the House of Commons.'

It was during that time that she met another Conservative MP, Richard Body. They married in 1959 and had a son and a daughter. Richard gave up politics for a while to return to the legal profession but in 1966 was re-elected as an MP and in 1985 knighted for political services, making his wife Lady Marion Body. Her husband's position as a prominent Eurosceptic often led to controversy.

'It's never been boring. The European issue has always been a big thing for him. He wasn't always toeing the party line, so it hasn't been dull.'

One area has never been a matter for debate between them so far as Marion is concerned. She has always refused to discuss her work at Bletchley with her husband.

'We knew we could never speak about it for the rest of our lives and even now I still find it rather difficult. It was thirty years after the war when that Winterbotham book was first published and Richard had been in Hatchards and he bought that book and came home with it and he came through the door and said: "Well, now will you tell me what you did during the war?" And I just said: "No."'

Colette St George-Yorke didn't know what to do with

herself after she left the Wrens. Eventually, she decided to go back to Harrogate to train as a State Registered Nurse, and then joined the Princess Mary's Royal Air Force Nursing Service.

'I hated being demobbed. I wanted to rejoin the forces. I wasn't old enough to join the naval nursing service as you had to be twenty-five, so I joined the RAF. Flying Officer St George-Yorke. It's the only time I've had a suit made to measure by a tailor in Mayfair.'

She married an RAF doctor, but he was posted to Iraq for two years and when he came back he seemed a changed person. She became pregnant with her son Peter but, for reasons she's never really understood, their marriage fell apart. In truth, he would always have been only second best. A part of her was still attached to Graham Murray, the handsome young pilot she lost during the war.

'He was a one-off. I'd moved on by the time I got married but I'd never forgotten him. You don't, you know. It was a long, long time after, but you never forget them, never.'

There is a small photograph in Colette's purse. A young man in RAF uniform is sat on the wooden platform of a tiny railway stop somewhere on a prairie in Canada. He looks tired. He's resting against a wooden trailer and alongside him are some milk churns. There's very little else to see in the picture – a single track and a line of telegraph poles stretching out into an endlessly flat distance. He's on his way to a training base to be taught how to drop agents behind enemy lines. On the back, that same young man has written: 'Waiting for a train en route to Moose Jaw 14th May 1942,' adding underneath: 'That's my parachute I'm sat on.' That's it. There is nothing more to the photograph, but it clearly hasn't stayed hidden away in the purse. The years of remembering have left a thousand tiny cracks across its once shiny surface.

In 2013, Colette's son Peter and his family took her to the war cemetery at Bergen-op-Zoom in Holland, just across the border from the spot in Belgium where Graham was shot down. For the first time, she saw his grave.

'It's the most peaceful place. I could have sat down there forever. It was the loveliest place ever. I don't know how people can forget. I only have to hear that music, Glenn Miller, "That Old Black Magic", and I'm back.'

Jane Fawcett has lived an astonishingly varied life. Looking back on it, and on her greatest memories, she is proud of performances as a professional singer. The fight to save the Midland Grand Hotel and other magnificent Victorian buildings, changing attitudes towards architecture along the way, was a great personal triumph for her as much as for her boss Sir Nikolaus Pevsner.

Jane had her own small personal role in the sinking of the *Bismarck*, but what of the codebreakers' other achievements, saving countless lives by predicting which cities the German bombers would attack each night, helping to sink the U-boats that were torpedoing the vital supplies from America?

Bletchley Park helped ensure victory in North Africa and Italy, and played a key role in the success of the D-Day landings. Without Bletchley, the D-Day deception operation that drastically cut the number of German troops confronting the Allies could not have gone ahead. The codebreakers also told Allied commanders what Hitler and his generals were thinking during the invasion, and as part of that process Bletchley Park became the birthplace of the electronic computer. The importance of the work done there during the Second World War is undeniable, but what does it mean to Jane? She's achieved a great deal in her life. Where does her own time at Bletchley rate among all of that?

'Singing has been the most personal thing, but I am also very passionate about saving great buildings, so both of those I was very happy to have, and of course I've been a mother and a grandmother, and that really comes top of the list.

'But as more and more evidence comes out about what Bletchley did, I've begun to realise that it was quite possibly the most important thing I did in my life. My contribution was minute, of course, but I gave all I had and it succeeded. We did win the war.'

Sources

Chapter 1

The National Archives (TNA) HW 3/135 Phoebe Senyard, 'The History of Miss Senyard's Party', German Naval Section BP; interviews and correspondence with Barbara Eachus (née Abernethy) from 1998 to 2003; interviews and correspondence with Diana Barraclough (née Russell-Clarke), May 1998; correspondence with Judie Hodsdon, daughter of Joan Bonsall (née Wingfield), 1 July 2014; private papers of Jocelyn Kerslake (née Bostock), kindly provided by her daughter Dr Celia Kerslake; interviews and correspondence with Ann Cunningham (née Lavell), May 1998 and 1999; interview with Gwen Watkins (née Davies) in 1998; Gwen Watkins, *Cracking the Luftwaffe Codes: The Secrets of Bletchley Park*, Greenhill Books, London, 2006.

Chapter 2

Interview with Jane Fawcett (née Hughes), July 2014; interviews and correspondence with Diana Barraclough (née Russell-Clarke), May 1998; Joy Ettridge (née

Higgins), *Hut 6 Bletchley Park* found at http://www.bbc.
co.uk/history/ww2peopleswar/stories/42/a4163942.
shtml; Imperial War Museum (IWM) Lyn Smith interview
with Pamela Bagnall (née Draughn), Catalogue Number
28456; Bletchley Park Archives (BPA) interview with Ailsa
Maxwell (née Macdonald); Mair and Gethin Russell-Jones,
*My Secret Life in Hut Six: One Woman's Experiences at Bletchley
Park*, Lion, Oxford, 2014.

Chapter 3

Interviews with Sarah 'Sally' Baring (née Norton), May
1998; BPA interview with Sarah Baring; Sarah Baring, *The
Road to Station X*, Wilton 65, York, 2000; private papers
of Jocelyn Kerslake (née Bostock); TNA HW 3/135 'The
History of Miss Senyard's Party'; interview with Harry
Hinsley, May 1995; conversations with Keith Batey, 1998
to 2010; interviews, conversations and correspondence
with Mavis Batey (née Lever), 1998 to 2013; interview
with Jane Fawcett (née Hughes), July 2014; F.H. Hinsley,
British Intelligence in the Second World War (Abridged
Edition), HMSO, London, 1994, pp54–8; TNA ADM
223/88 Admiralty Use of Special Intelligence in Naval
Operations, pp53–73; ADM 223/464 Wireless intelligence
and the Bismarck, p139; interview with Jim and Pamela
Rose (née Gibson), May 1998; Jean Campbell-Harris
from Jean Trumpington, *Coming Up Trumps: A Memoir*,
Macmillan, London, 2014; Anne de Courcy, *Debs at War:
How Wartime Changed Their Lives 1939–1945*, Weidenfeld
and Nicolson, 2005; BPA interview with Evelyn Margaret
'Peggy' Senior; interview with Valerie Emery (née Travis),

1998; BPA interview with Sheila Lawn (née Mackenzie); BPA interview with Jean Tocher.

Chapter 4
Interview with Morag Beatty (née Maclennan), 1998; interview with Colette Cook (née St George-Yorke), June 2014; interview with Anne Hill (née Zuppinger), 1998; Gwendoline Page (Ed.), *We Kept the Secret: Enigma Memories*, Reeve, Wymondham, 2002; interview with Barbara Quirk, 1998; interview with Joan Baily (née Read), 1998.

Chapter 5
Interview with Jane Fawcett (née Hughes), July 2014; Mair and Gethin Russell-Jones, *My Secret Life in Hut Six*; interview with Christine Brooke-Rose, May 1998; Christine Brooke-Rose, *Remake*, Carcanet, Manchester, 1996; interviews and correspondence with Barbara Eachus (née Abernethy) from 1998 to 2003; interview with Jean Howard (née Alington), 1998; IWM Private Papers of Mrs J. Howard 12132; IWM Lyn Smith interview with Pamela Bagnall (née Draughn); interviews and correspondence with Ann Cunningham (née Lavell), May 1998 and 1999; BPA interview with Barbara Mulligan.

Chapter 6
TNA HW 3/135 'The History of Miss Senyard's Party'; interview with Pat Bing (née Wright), June 1998; BBC, *Horizon*, 'The Strange Life and Death of Dr Turing', 1992; Joan Clarke, 'Hut 8 and Naval Enigma Part I', in F.H. Hinsley and Alan Stripp, *Codebreakers: The Inside Story of*

Bletchley Park, OUP, Oxford, 1993; Ralph Erskine, 'Murray [Clarke], Joan Elisabeth Lowther (1917–1996)', *Oxford Dictionary of National Biography*, Oxford University Press, 2004; TNA ADM 223/464, Operation Ruthless; Hinsley, *British Intelligence in the Second World War*; BPA interview with Eileen Johnson (née Plowman); interview with Morag Beatty (née Maclennan), 1998; BPA interview with Mrs N.G. Edwards (née Harrison); interview with Shaun Wylie, May 1998; Page, *We Kept the Secret*; TNA HW 64/75 GC&CS Women's Committee.

Chapter 7

Interviews, conversations and correspondence with Mavis Batey (née Lever), 1998 to 2013; Mavis Batey, *Dilly: The Man Who Broke Enigmas*, Biteback, London, 2009; Kerry Howard, *Dear Codebreaker: The Letters of Margaret and John Rock*, BookTower, Redditch, 2013; interview with Helen Jean Pitt-Lewis (née Orme), October 2014; TNA WO 208/3575 Williams, 'The Use of Ultra'.

Chapter 8

Interview with Sarah 'Sally' Baring (née Norton), 1998; Mair and Gethin Russell-Jones, *My Secret Life in Hut Six*; BPA interview with Mrs A. Mitchell (née Williamson); B. Jack Copeland and others, *Colossus: The Secrets of Bletchley Park's Codebreaking Computers*, OUP, Oxford, 2006; interview with Marigold Freeman-Attwood (née Philips), July 2014; BPA interview with Mrs Margaret 'Maggie' Mortimer (née Broughton-Thompson); interview with Jean Harvey (née Thompson), 1998; interview with Shaun and Odette Wylie (née Murray), 1998; IWM Lyn Smith interview with Pamela Bagnall (née Draughn); interview and correspondence with Susan Wenham 1998–99.

Chapter 9

Interview with Mary Every (née Wisbey), August 2014; Elizabeth Hawken, *Recollections of Bletchley Park*, unpublished memoirs kindly provided by her daughter Miss S.C.J. Hawken; interview with Marjorie Halcrow, 1998; conversations and correspondence with Rosemary Merry (née Calder), July 1999, February 2000; interview and correspondence with Olive Hirst (née Humble), July 1999, November 2000 and October 2014; correspondence with Dorothy Smith (née Robertson), February and April 1999; interviews with Betty Webb (née Vine-Stevens), July 1999, January 2000, April 2014; interview with Gladys Sweetland, February 2000; interview with Lady Marion Body (née Graham), May 2014.

Chapter 10

Sarah Baring, *The Road to Station X*; interview with Colette Cook (née St George-Yorke), June 2014; interview with Roma Davies (née Stenning), June 2014; correspondence with Dorothy Smith (née Robertson), February and April 1999; interviews and correspondence with Barbara Eachus (née Abernethy) from 1998 to 2003; interviews with Betty Webb (née Vine-Stevens), July 1999, January 2000, April 2014; letter from Julie Lydekker, May 1999; TNA HW 3/135 'The History of Miss Senyard's Party'; interviews, conversations and correspondence with Mavis Batey (née

Lever), 1998 to 2013; Ralph Erskine, 'Murray [Clarke], Joan Elisabeth Lowther (1917–1996)', *Oxford Dictionary of National Biography*; Kerry Howard, *Dear Codebreaker*; interview with Jane Fawcett (née Hughes), July 2014; interview with Marigold Freeman-Attwood (née Philips), July 2014; Joy Ettridge (née Higgins), *Hut 6 Bletchley Park*; BPA interview with Mrs Margaret 'Maggie' Mortimer (née Broughton-Thompson); interview with Mary Every (née Wisbey), August 2014; Mair and Gethin Russell-Jones, *My Secret Life in Hut Six*; interview and correspondence with Susan Wenham, 1998–99; interviews and correspondence with Olive Hirst (née Humble), July 1999, November 2000 and October 2014; obituary of Christine Brooke-Rose, *Independent*, 27 March 2012; interview with Lady Marion Body (née Graham), May 2014.

Bibliography

For the General Reader

Sarah Baring, *The Road to Station X* (Wilton, 2000)

Mavis Batey, *Dilly: The Man Who Broke Enigmas* (Biteback, 2009)

Asa Briggs, *Secret Days: Codebreaking in Bletchley Park: A Memoir of Hut Six and the Enigma Machine* (Frontline Books, 2011)

Christine Brooke-Rose, *Remake* (Carcanet, 1996)

Jean Chitty, *Kent House Colombo: Letters from a Wren, May 1944 to November 1945* (Belhaven, 1994)

Anne de Courcy, *Debs at War: How Wartime Changed Their Lives 1939–1945* (Weidenfeld and Nicolson, 2005)

Tessa Dunlop, *The Bletchley Girls* (Hodder & Stoughton, 2015)

Marion Hill, *Bletchley Park People: Churchill's Geese that Never Cackled* (The History Press, 2004)

Kerry Howard, *Dear Codebreaker: The Letters of Margaret and John Rock* (BookTower Publishing, 2013)

Kerry Howard, *Women Codebreakers at Bletchley Park* (BookTower Publishing, 2015)

Anne Lewis-Smith, *Off Duty! Bletchley Park Outstation Gayhurst Manor* (Traeth, 2006)

Doreen Luke, *My Road to Bletchley Park* (M. & M. Baldwin, 2003)

Sinclair McKay, *The Lost World of Bletchley Park: The Illustrated History of the Wartime Codebreaking Centre* (Aurum, 2013)

Sinclair McKay, *The Secret Life of Bletchley Park* (Aurum, 2010)

Sinclair McKay, *The Secret Listeners: How the Wartime Y Service Intercepted the Secret German Codes for Bletchley Park* (Aurum, 2013)

Hugh Melinsky, *A Code-breaker's Tale* (Larks Press, 1998)

Gwendoline Page, *Growing Pains: A Teenager's War* (Book Guild, 1994)

Gwendoline Page, *They Listened in Secret* (Reeve, 2003)

Gwendoline Page (Ed.), *We Kept the Secret: Enigma Memories* (Reeve, 2002)

Mair and Gethin Russell-Jones, *My Secret Life in Hut Six: One Woman's Experiences at Bletchley Park* (Lion, 2014)

Hugh Sebag-Montefiore, *Enigma: The Battle for the Code* (Cassell, 2004)

Elisa Segrave, *The Girl from Station X: My Mother's Unknown Life* (Aurum, 2013)

Phil Shanahan, *The Real Enigma Heroes* (The History Press, 2010)

Michael Smith, *Bletchley Park: The Code-Breakers of Station X* (Shire, 2013)

Michael Smith, *Britain's Secret War 1939–45: How Espionage, Codebreaking and Covert Operations Helped Win the War* (Andre Deutsch, 2011)

Michael Smith, *Station X: The Code Breakers of Bletchley Park* (Pan, 2004)

Michael Smith, *The Emperor's Codes: Bletchley Park's Role in the War Against Japan* (Biteback, 2009)

Michael Smith, *The Secrets of Station X: How the Bletchley Park Codebreakers Helped Win the War* (Biteback, 2011)

James Thirsk, *Bletchley Park: An Inmate's Story* (M. & M. Baldwin, 2012)

Jean Trumpington, *Coming Up Trumps: A Memoir* (Macmillan, 2014)

Gwen Watkins, *Cracking the Luftwaffe Codes, The Secrets of Bletchley Park* (Greenhill, 2006)

Charlotte Webb, *Secret Postings: Bletchley Park to the Pentagon* (BookTower Publishing, 2011)

Irene Young, *Enigma Variations: Love, War and Bletchley Park* (Mainstream, 2000)

For the Enthusiast

Ralph Bennett, *Behind the Battle: Intelligence in the War with Germany 1939–1945* (Pimlico, 1999)

Ralph Bennett, *Ultra and Mediterranean Strategy 1941–45* (Hamish Hamilton, 1989)

Ralph Bennett, *Ultra in the West: The Normandy Campaign of 1944–45* (Hutchinson, 1979)

Stephen Budiansky, *Battle of Wits: The Complete Story of Codebreaking in World War II* (Viking, 2000)

Peter Calvocoressi, *Top Secret Ultra* (M. & M. Baldwin, 2011)

B. Jack Copeland and others, *Colossus: The Secrets of Bletchley Park's Codebreaking Computers* (OUP, 2010)

Robin Denniston, *Thirty Secret Years: A.G. Denniston's Work in Signals Intelligence 1914–1944* (Polperro Heritage Press, 2007)

Peter Donovan and John Mack, *Code Breaking in the Pacific* (Springer, 2014)

Ralph Erskine and Michael Smith (Eds), *The Bletchley Park Codebreakers* (Biteback, 2011)

Joel Greenburg, *Gordon Welchman: Bletchley Park's Architect of Ultra Intelligence* (Frontline, 2014)

Christopher Grey, *Decoding Organization: Bletchley Park, Codebreaking and Organization Studies* (CUP, 2013)

John Herivel, *Herivelismus and the German Military Enigma* (M. & M. Baldwin, 2008)

F.H. Hinsley, *British Intelligence in the Second World War* (Abridged Edition) (HMSO, 1994)

F.H. Hinsley and Alan Stripp (Eds), *Codebreakers: The Inside Story of Bletchley Park* (OUP, 2001)

Andrew Hodges, *Alan Turing: The Enigma* (Vintage, 2014)

John Jackson (ed.), *Solving Enigma's Secrets: The Official History of Bletchley Park's Hut 6* (BookTower Publishing, 2014)

John Johnson, *The Evolution of British Sigint 1653–1939* (GCHQ, 1997)

Kerry Johnson and John Gallehawk, *Figuring It Out at Bletchley Park 1939–1945* (BookTower Publishing, 2007)

David Kahn, *Seizing the Enigma: The Race to Break the German U-boat Codes 1939-1943* (Arrow, 1996)

David Kahn, *The Codebreakers* (Weidenfeld and Nicolson, 1974)

Ronald Lewin, *Ultra Goes to War* (Penguin, 2001)

Joss Pearson, *Cribs for Victory: The Untold Story of Bletchley Park's Secret Room* (Polperro Heritage Press, 2011)

Geoffrey Pidgeon, *The Secret Wireless War* (UPSO, 2007)

Fred Piper and Sean Murphy, *Cryptography: A Very Short Introduction* (OUP, 2002)

Simon Singh, *Code Book* (4th Estate, 1999)

Alan Stripp, *Codebreaker in the Far East* (Frank Cass, 1989)

John Stubbington, *Kept in the Dark: The Denial to Bomber Command of Vital Ultra and Other Intelligence Information During World War II* (Pen and Sword, 2010)

Gordon Welchman, *The Hut Six Story: Breaking the Enigma Codes* (M. & M. Baldwin, 1997)

Nigel West, *GCHQ: The Secret Wireless War 1900–86* (Weidenfeld and Nicolson, 1986)

Frederick Winterbotham, *The Ultra Secret* (Weidenfeld and Nicolson, 1974)

Acknowledgements

The story of the women who worked at Bletchley Park is an astonishing part of our wartime history. At its peak in May 1945, 10,500 people worked at Bletchley, over 7,000 of them women. They are all too often dismissed as tiny cogs in a big machine, not least with commendable modesty by themselves. But this misses the point. Quite apart from the fact that several of the top codebreakers were women, everyone who worked at Bletchley Park played a role in its many achievements. They helped keep the vital supply lines across the Atlantic open, saved the lives of untold numbers of civilians during the Blitz, helped ensure the victories in North Africa and Italy and, most importantly, the success of the D-Day invasion. As if that weren't enough, Bletchley Park was also the birthplace of the modern electronic computer. I am grateful to everyone who helped tell their story, in particular the very many female veterans I have interviewed over the years, a number of whom have sadly since died.

My particular thanks go to those featured in this

book: Pamela Bagnall; Joan Baily; Sarah Baring; Diana Barraclough; Morag Beatty; Pat Bing; Lady Marion Body; Christine Brooke-Rose; Colette Cook; Ann Cunningham; Barbara Eachus; Nancy Edwards; Valerie Emery; Mary Every; Jane Fawcett; Marigold Freeman-Attwood; Jean Harvey; Anne Hill; Olive Hirst; Jean Howard; Eileen Johnson; Sheila Lawn; Ailsa Maxwell; Rosemary Merry; Ann Mitchell; Maggie Mortimer; Barbara Mulligan; Gwendoline Page; Jean Pitt-Lewis; Pamela Rose; Peggy Senior; Dorothy Smith; Gladys Sweetland; Jean Tocher; Gwen Watkins; Betty Webb; Susan Wenham; Odette Wylie; and in particular the late Mavis Batey who more than any other individual was the inspiration behind this book. I am extremely grateful to the staff and volunteers of the Bletchley Park Trust, including Jonathan Byrne, Kelsey Griffin, Vicky Worpole, Gillian Mason, Richard Lewis and Sarah Kay, for their generous assistance and their willingness to share their interviews with veterans with me; the staff of the National Archives and the Imperial War Museum for their courtesy and patience; the long-suffering editorial team at Aurum, Iain MacGregor (whose idea this book was), Jennifer Barr, Lucy Warburton, Charlotte Coulthard, Ian Allen and Liz Somers. Thanks are also due to Sarah Hawken, Celia Kerslake, Peter Barnes and Judie Hodsdon, to Robert Kirby and Holly Thompson, and last but by no means least to my wife Hayley for her unfailing support.

Michael Smith, October 2014

Index